William of Nassington

American University Studies

Series VII
Theology and Religion
Vol. 19

PETER LANG
New York · Berne · Frankfurt am Main

Ingrid J. Peterson

WILLIAM OF NASSINGTON

Canon, Mystic, and Poet of the *Speculum Vitae*

PETER LANG
New York · Berne · Frankfurt am Main

Library of Congress Cataloging-in-Publication Data

Peterson, Ingrid J.
  William of Nassington : Canon, Mystic, and Poet of the Speculum vitae.

  (American University Studies. Series VII, Theology and Religion ; vol. 19)
    Bibliography : p.
    Includes index.
    1. William, of Nassington. 2. William, of Nassington. Speculum vitae. 3. Lord's prayer—Early works to 1800. 4. Vices—Early works to 1800. 5. Virtues—Early works to 1800. I. Title. II. Series : American University Studies. Series VII, Theology and Religion ; v. 19.
  BX4705.W558P47   1986   241'.3   86-18544
  ISBN 0-8204-0322-9
  ISSN 0740-0446

CIP-Kurztitelaufnahme der Deutschen Bibliothek

Peterson, Ingrid J.:
William of Nassington : Canon, Mystic, and Poet of the Speculum vitae / Ingrid J. Peterson. –
New York ; Berne ; Frankfurt am Main : Lang, 1986.
  (American University Studies : Ser. 7, Theology and Religion ; Vol. 19)
  ISBN 0-8204-0322-9

NE: American University Studies / 07

© Peter Lang Publishing, Inc., New York 1986

All rights reserved.
Reprint or reproduction, even partially, in all forms such as microfilm, xerography, microfiche, microcard, offset strictly prohibited.

Printed by Weihert-Druck GmbH, Darmstadt (West Germany)

To Hope Emily Allen

TABLE OF CONTENTS

Page

CHAPTER

I. THE NASSINGTONS IN THE LATE MEDIEVAL CHURCH 1

    The Reform Movement in the English Church 2
    Administrative Structure of the English Church 7
    The Nassington Family Administrators 12
    William of Nassington: Priest and Poet 17

II. AUTHORSHIP, DATE, AND PROVENANCE OF THE
SPECULUM VITAE 39

    Authorship of the Speculum Vitae 40
    Manuscript Dates and Circulation 46
    Literary Backgrounds and Imputed Sources 50

III. THE SPECULUM VITAE AS A DIDACTIC COMPENDIUM 77

    The Structure and Organization of the Speculum Vitae . . 81
    First Exposition of the Pater Noster Petitions
    (98-2294) 84
    Second Exposition of the Petitions of the Pater
    Noster (2295-3306) 88
    Third Exposition of the Petitions of the Pater
    Noster (3307-16,396) 94
    Nassington's Narration on the Vice of Avarice 103

IV. THE SPECULUM VITAE AS A MANUAL OF PERFECTION 111

    The Beginning Process of Purgation 115
    The Intermediate Process of Illumination 122
    Mystical Union as the Goal of Perfection
    (13,225-16,395) 136

V. MINOR WORKS ATTRIBUTED TO NASSINGTON 149

    The Cotton Tiberius Manuscript 155
    St. Marys Lamentation to St. Bernard 158
    The Form of Living 160
    Spiritus Guydonis 163

CHAPTER	Page
VI. CONCLUSION	169
BIBLIOGRAPHY	175
INDEX	189

PREFACE

Baugh's Literary History of England, questions the date, author, and source of the Speculum Vitae. My research provides evidence to resolve these uncertainties. Chapter I establishes Nassington's identity, Chapter II his dates and sources, and Chapter V his canon. The biographical data I have amassed, following the direction set by Hope Emily Allen's scholarship, on William of Nassington and his ecclesiastical family in York indicates that he is the author of the Speculum Vitae. My discovery of the transcription of Archbishop Zouche's appointment of Nassington in 1354 from Exeter as York Official and visitor resolves the crux of his identity. The dates of Nassington's life correspond with the certificate in MMS. Cambridge Il.i., Bodleian 445, and Caius College 160 which establishes 1384 as the terminus ad quem for the Speculum Vitae.

Chapters III and IV, a textual analysis of the Speculum Vitae, indicate that it is a didactic work drawing its theology and structure from traditional sources--Augustine, Gregory of Nyssa, Ambrose, Irenaeus, Hilary, Cyprian, Tertullian, Origen, and Thomas. Nassington's synthesis of patristic doctrine meets the demands of the reform movement. This doctrine is also the foundation for his treatment of the three stages of spiritual growth, disclosing the prayerful insight of his rich interior life. The autobiographical traces of Nassington, as mystic touched by moments of lyric prayer, especially in response to the grace of the Gifts of the Holy Spirit, are identifiable in the Tractatus de Trinitate et Unitate, but not in the other minor poems which Horstmann originally ascribed to Nassington. The colophon in MSS. Royal 17. C. viii and Hatton 19 attributing the Speculum Vitae to Nassington and the incipits in MS. B. L. Additional 33995, naming Nassington as author of the Trinitate, are manuscript evidence to verify his canon.

William of Nassington is a scholar and original thinker who assimilated a summa of doctrine and a treatise on moral perfection into the Speculum Vitae. Nassington is a speculum of orthodox religious England, and the Speculum Vitae, because of its popularity, needs to be recognized along with the great fourteenth century mystical writings.

I am grateful for the encouragement of Professor Valerie Lagorio whose enthusiasm for the English mystics led me to focus my doctoral studies on William of Nassington and his Speculum Vitae. I am indebted to the academic communities at the University of Iowa and the College of Saint Teresa, Winona, Minnesota. I wish to thank my family, friends, and the Sisters of St. Francis, Rochester, Minnesota, for their support and assistance.

CHAPTER I

THE NASSINGTONS IN THE LATE MEDIEVAL CHURCH

The identity of William of Nassington and his authorship of various religious works have been elusive critical problems of medieval scholarship. Records of his widespread church activity in both the southern diocese of Exeter and the northern diocese of York misled his critics to conclude that there were two, or even six, Williams of Nassington. He has been imputed to be the author, not only of the Speculum Vitae, but of the Prick of Conscience, the minor poems in MS. B. L. Cotton Tiberius E. VII, which includes a verse form of Richard Rolle's Form of Living, and the expanded Northern Homily collection. Moreover, erroneous sources have been assigned to him. For example, the Speculum Vitae was described as a derivative of John Waldeby's Mirror of Life until Hope Emily Allen in 1917 discovered such a text to be nonexistent. His name often appears in medieval scholarship, such as Wells' Manual and Brown and Robbins' Index, but the text of his Speculum Vitae was not available until 1977. His minor poems were included in Horstmann's Yorkshire Writers: Richard Rolle and His Followers (1896). Nassington's elusiveness as a cleric and poet, and my growing curiosity about him, led me to investigate the critical problems surrounding his identity, his canon of work, his sources, and in particular his relationship to Waldeby and the significance of his work as the culmination of two centuries of religious writing in the medieval English church.

In order to understand the importance of Nassington and his work, it is necessary to examine the English religious temper of the thirteenth and fourteenth centuries, the structure of the English church, and the long and distinguished lineage of Nassington ecclesiastics. This period, beginning with the Fourth Lateran Council, is marked by an unusual effort toward the moral reform of the clergy and increased emphasis on the instruction of both clergy and laity in the faith. The reform in England was shaped by diocesan councils and synods, which, in addition to legislating against moral laxity and ignorance, clarified questions of essential doctrinal belief and minimal sacramental participation for the laity. Corresponding with, and possibly as a result of these reform movements, there was a surge of interest in the devotional life and in mysticism among the faithful.

The Reform Movement in the English Church

The Fourth Lateran Council of 1215, convoked by Pope Innocent III, marked the beginning of one of the most energetic reforms in the history of the church. It was attended by 1,300 prelates from the Western church, legislating seventy canons that confirmed earlier disciplinary procedures and established as minimal requirements for church membership annual auricular confession and communion.[1]

In England the papal reforms of the council were promulgated and implemented through 23 diocesan synods held between 1219 and 1268.[2] Following the council's directive, the diocesan synods published the results of their legislation, thus fulfilling their pastoral duty to instruct the faithful, including the clergy.

It should be noted that this practice of circulating papal canons in writing had been followed in the early Middle Ages, but by the twelfth century, judging from the void in the records, it must have ceased. Accordingly, in 1222, Stephen Langton, Archbishop of Canterbury (1151-1228), convoked synods, or dioceasan meetings, to adapt the canonical decrees of the Fourth Lateran Council to English localities. Some of the specific abuses addressed by these synodal decrees were: neglect of pastoral care and sacramental ministry, acceptance of church offices as sinecures, simony in the form of selling church offices, immorality, and worldliness.

Under this scheme for reform, the papal canons, especially those dealing with confession and absolution, were transmitted as "statutes" by the diocesan synods and their provinces to the clergy and lay people.[3] Not content with publishing and glossing these statutes, individual English bishops of the thirteenth century added to them, making "constitutions." A primary example of these writings was the pastoral Constitutiones of Robert Grosseteste, Bishop of Lincoln (1235-1253), which was one of the most influential and widely disseminated texts, and which contained decrees specifically directed to the parochial clergy of his diocese. Grosseteste's <u>Constitutiones</u> were used for more than 200 years, and provided the chief outline of doctrinal instruction that was directed toward the English clergy and laity until the end of the Middle Ages. In a further effort to enlighten his people, Grossesteste also wrote the <u>Templum Domini</u>, an elaborate archetypal manual on confession for parish priests, which treated the ten commandments, vices and virtues, and sacraments.[4]

Another example of "constitutions," generated by the Provincial Council of Lambeth in 1281, was Archbishop John Pecham's <u>De informatione simplicium</u>, which begins by declaring: "The ignorance of the clergy casts the people into the pit of error. . ." It, too, presents a systematic course of instruction for the laity:

> Four times a year, that is, once in each quarter of the year, on one or more holy days each priest presiding over the people, himself or through another person, shall explain to the people in their everyday language, without the fantastic web of any kind of subtlety, the fourteen articles of faith; the ten commandmants of the decalogue; the two precepts of the gospel, namely, the twin sisters of charity; the seven works of mercy; the seven capital sins with their progeny; the seven principal virtues; and the seven sacraments of grace.[5]

Pecham's decree was largely a schema, with little exposition and commentary. The elementary knowledge of the Christian faith that the priest was directed to impart, and which he himself might not have, was not contained in this decree. While it warned against ignorance, it was not a manual of practical theology to combat ignorance. It presumed rather than imparted knowledge, and demanded a companion volume of practical theology, such as Grosseteste's Templum Domini.[6]

A third influential work addressed to clergy or members of the laity for their private devotion, or for their use as a spiritual guide, was St. Edmund Rich's Speculum Ecclesiae, which later was translated into Anglo-Norman and English.[7] This popular work of instruction in the way of perfection outlines a doctrinal program which corresponded to the topics in Pecham's Lambeth decree: the seven deadly sins, seven virtues, seven gifts of the Holy Spirit, ten commandments, twelve articles of faith, seven sacraments, seven works of mercy, seven prayers of the Pater Noster, and the joys of heaven and pains of hell. Rich wrote that to love honorably, to know oneself, and to contemplate God in his creatures and in the Scriptures would lead the devout to perfection, thereby pointing the way for subsequent fourteenth-century manuals.

Beginning with the provincial councils of Oxford in 1222, canons, statutes, and constitutions were frequently copied, and if an archbishop found them adequate, he simply renewed the same legislation and promulgated it again to his clergy.[8] One fourteenth-century document, the Summa Summarum, included provincial statutes from Oxford in 1222, Reading in 1269, and the later councils of Lambeth in 1261 and 1281. Thus recording conciliar legislation and compiling the material into compendia established a model for writing compilations drawn from many sources. The clerical hierarchy and ecclesiastical lawyers came to depend upon such compendia of legislation in matter of appointments, discipline, and religious practice.

The importance of the written texts of such synodal legislation lessened in the fourteenth century when English bishops began to communicate to their people and instruct them through pastoral letters.[9] As a result, manuals of religious instruction became the work of religious educators other than bishops. Cathedral churches, monastic houses, and the universities of Oxford and Cambridge became important centers producing such writings of religious instruction. The archdiocese of York became a center of intellectual activity, where the Austin friars had one of the finest libraries in England, and where John Waldeby, one of the best preachers and letter writers of the later fourteenth century, gave courses in sermons.[10]

This time of institutional and personal renewal in the church also produced the great English mystics of the fourteenth century: Richard Rolle, the anonymous author of The Cloud of Unknowing and its cognate tracts, Walter Hilton, Julian of Norwich, and Margery Kempe. Nassington's Speculum Vitae is an ascetical and mystical text that follows in the direct tradition of these outstanding English mystics. The written accounts of English mystical experience such as Rolle's Melos Amoris or Incendium Amoris and Julian of Norwich's Revelations of Divine Love, suggest the rich inner life experienced by many clerics, religious, and devout laity. The purpose of the writings of the mystics was to prepare the faithful for contemplation and its fruit, prophetic social action. Following in Rich's footsteps, the English mystics provided guides to meditation, which they described as the systematic reflection on a truth or passage of Scripture that instructed the mind, moved the will, and disposed the heart for prayer. They taught that meditation was the first step toward the life of higher prayer. The basic principle behind all contemplation was that God, though ineffable, was knowable through his revelation in Christ, the God-man, on whom the faithful could concentrate with intense feeling and tenderness.

All of these developments--the Roman papal councils, English synods and provincial councils, pastoral constitutions, spiritual renewal, and rise of mysticism--produced a literature of instructional, devotional writing, whose chief aim was to systematize religious knowledge by the scholastic method of definition, division, and its transmission to the faithful.

Administrative Structure of the English Church

The reforms of the Fourth Latern Council were directed to the church, not only as a body of worshipping believers but also as a governing structure. Concomitant with the moral reforms and emphasis upon instruction of the clergy and faithful was an increased centralization of church administration, resulting in an increasingly autonomous institution in England. The English monarchy and the centralized Roman church were analogous in administrative organization as well as in their efforts to upgrade the intellectual, spiritual, and social lives of the people.[11] The dioceses of Canterbury and York, while independent of each other, were the most influential church centers in England.

Owing to the close tie of church and crown, especially in appointments to ecclesiastical positions, administrative offices often had political and secular significance, resulting in ecclesiastical civil service. Pantin describes a "civil-servant bishop" as one who held office in the service of the crown before becoming bishop, or one who simultaneously held political and episcopal offices.[12] The increasing frequency of this practice was evident in the seventeen English bishoprics: in 1300, two bishops were civil servants; in 1325, twelve; in 1350, eight; and 1374, ten bishops were civil servants. By 1400, however, as the church became more independent of the state, the number of civil-servant bishops began to decline. Pantin suggests that to trace the history of the tenth, eleventh, or twelfth-century bishops, one should consult the monastic chronicles, the writings in Patrologia Latina, or Butler's Lives of the Saints, but in order to find the background of fourteenth-century English bishops, one would look for civil leaders, who are found in Tout's chapters in the Administrative History of Medieval England.

King John granted and Pope Innocent III confirmed what had been the practice since the beginning of Christianity in England, namely, that the state not interfere with the appointments of bishops,[13] but his law was loosely interpreted. For after the election of a bishop by a diocesan synod, the appointee had to be approved by the king. If the king considered the candidate an enemy, foreigner, or unsatisfactory in any way, he could refuse to appoint the elected bishop. When endorsed by the king, the bishop received royal patronage so that high administrative positions in the church brought with them benefices from the crown, or offices endowed with fixed capital holdings.

Under the bishop each diocese was an independent entity, and the administrative hierarchy within each diocese was under his direct control. The most influential bishops of the English medieval church were leaders with theological training and administrative ability, such as Bishop Robert Grosseteste of Lincoln and John Pecham of Canterbury, who were illustrious magistri prior to their episcopal appointments. Bishops resided in cathedral complexes, and were assisted by the following dignitaries: the dean, who was the head of the chapter; the precentor, a member of the chapter second to the dean, who served as a director of the choir; the treasurer; and the chancellor, or official secretary, who also made visitations. Each bishop also appointed a body of canons who recited the ecclesiastical hours. The bishop normally appointed his own canons and archdeacons, while the dean of the cathedral chapter was elected by the diocescan chapter.[14]

It is true that the bishop was the highest governing officer of his diocese, but his frequent absence to conduct royal business and to make visitations to the religious houses and churches in his diocese compelled him to appoint two administrative officers to carry on his work: the vicar general, who held the chief administrative power and the seal of the bishop in his absence, and the "official," who was his judicial representative. Toward the end of the thirteenth century, as English bishops were more frequently absent from their sees, the vicar general functioned with all the jurisdiction of the bishop. If the bishop had to assume the administration of an additional diocese left vacant by the death of another bishop, he gave authority to govern his own diocese to this official. Under the administration of Archbishop Greenfield (1304-1315), these two offices of vicar general and official merged so that one person was appointed to hold the power of both offices.[15]

In addition to the cathedral church, each English diocese also supported collegiate churches, or those which did not have a cathedral. The average collegiate church or minster contained within its boundaries seven or eight prebendal foundations, or small divisions with an income from a trust, to which were assigned a priest canon or rector. Although each canon was appointed by the bishop, he was supported by the landowner of the property and performed pastoral duties for the prebend. As the thirteenth century progressed and landowners grew wealthy and were able to increase the endowments attached to the prebends, the canon priests began to employ stipendary priests as "vicars" for their ministerial and liturgical duties. Each canon could employ two vicars, one for the regular liturgical and sacramental duties, the other to minister to the pastoral need of the parish.[16] This arrangement freed the canon from his ministerial duties, permitting him to live wherever he chose on his prebendal income. As a result, priest canons often became detached from the worshipping laity.

Appointments of parish clergy in collegiate churches and parishes varied in the church in England,[17] but "hired clergy," who may not have been prepared for pastoral duties, outnumbered beneficed clergy, who were supported directly from their prebendal income. Some clergy assigned to the parish actually served the people who supported them, while others, called pluralists, received salaries from more than one benefice and did not reside within the parish or prebend boundaries. Often clergy who resided in their parishes and worked for whatever small stipend the landowner of the benefice could contribute lived simple lives of dedication to their people, such as Chaucer's exemplar, the "pore persoun." When ordained clergy could not be found to serve as vicars, clerks and other clergy in minor orders were hired. All were paid on a low scale, and often their private standards of manners and morals were not very high. John Myrk's <u>Instructions for Parish Priests</u> (1420) specifically addressed these clergy, informing them of doctrine and moral principles.[18]

Parish clergy varied in social class from the wealthy, called by canon law "sublime and literate persons,"[19] to rank-and-file untrained clerics. In general, the training of clergy in the Middle Ages was not very thorough, for it must be remembered that the systematic formation and education of clergy did not begin until the Council of Trent in 1545.[20] Some clergy went to Oxford and Cambridge for a few years, and some stayed long enough to receive university degrees. Those who excelled academically were usually employed as administrators, theologians, and canon lawyers in the cathedral church. Other clergy who did not attend a university could be trained in the cathedral or monastic schools or apprenticed to senior priests, or self-educated by means of the manuals designed for the clergy, or by a combination of these methods. Religious compilations of the fourteenth century, such as the <u>Speculum Vitae</u>, contained essential matters of doctrine and devotion to help prepare the less educated clergy for their obligation to instruct others in faith.

The Nassington Family Administrators

Against this background of reform in the English church stood the illustrious family of the Nassingtons in Yorkshire, astute ecclesiastics whose university education and experience in the law courts of both church and state prepared them to function in the most powerful diocesan offices. While their relationships are uncertain, the Nassingtons as officials and vicars general were the deputies of the bishop except for ordination and confirmation, exclusively episcopal duties.[21] Upon the death of the bishop, they were also appointed <u>sede vacante</u>, to assume the jurisdiction of the empty see. In these positions, they convened and conducted diocesan synods, made <u>ad hoc</u> diocesan visitations, presided over elections in religious houses, received monies due the bishopric, procured oaths of obedience from prebends, and issued dispensations for clergy who elected not to reside in the church where they received an income.[22] The career of William of Nassington continued a long family tradition of such service to the fourteenth-century English church.

John Nassington, whose career sets a pattern for the other Nassington administrators, was the official of York under five successive archbishops: John Romeyn (1285-1296), Henry Newark (1296-1299), Thomas Corbridge (1299-1304), William Greenfield (1304-1315), and William Melton (1316-1340). While no single person can be credited with the system of keeping diocesan registers, A. Hamilton Thompson, an English church historian, suggests that John Nassington may be most responsible, since the earliest surviving records appear at the time he immigrated from Lincoln with Romeyn.[23] Not only for the official, but for other members of the administration, an efficient system of recording official correspondence and activities of the diocese was necessary. These diocesan registers, together with the royal patent and close rolls, are the paramount source for accounts of the Nassington appointments and clearly indicate the eminence of the family.[24]

The meteoric ascendancy of John Nassington (d. 1317) in the archdiocese of York typifies the diversity of the ecclesiastical and civil service careers of the Nassingtons. John's first appointment under Archbishop John Romeyn was as rector of Kendal, Westmoreland, in 1296.[25] In 1300, while still a deacon, he was appointed as official of York prior to the election of Archbishop William Greenfield.[26] In 1305 he became a civil servant when he was appointed under Edward I as king's clerk. He remained as official of York under Greenfield, who also appointed him as vicar general, thus combining the powers of the two highest offices under the archbishop.[27] During this entire period he was liberally supported by benefices, for he held appointments as ecclesiastical canon of Beverley and York with prebends of St. Martin's altar, South Newbold, Bole and Wistow.[28] He died in 1317 after 21 years of service.[29]

The records of John Nassington, Junior (d. 1334), are difficult to separate from those of his father and from yet another John who was a member of the ecclesiastical court of York and was appointed official of York in 1316.[30] The younger John was granted a license to study in 1312, and promoted to clerical orders in 1314.[31] In 1320, he was given a papal benefice, granted by Ramsey Abbey in the Huntingdon diocese. He served widely in the dioceses of York, Lincoln, Exeter, Devon, and Barnstable.

Archbishop Grandisson (1327-1369) appointed him as chancellor of Exeter in 1328. He was made archdeacon of Barnstable in 1330 and archdeacon of Stowe in 1333, offices culminating 22 years of service.

Robert Nassington (d. 1345) began his career in 1324 when he received the title magister, probably from Oxford.[32] In 1329 he was granted a papal benefice as a gift of the archbishop and chapter of York. He was appointed in 1332 as precentor of York, a position he held until his death in 1345.[33] During his 21 years of service, he received appointments as acolyte, rector, and ecclesiastical canon and prebend. In 1333 Archbishop William Melton appointed him as vicar general, the judicial head of the diocesan tribunal, thus making him the highest power in the diocese next to the bishop.[34]

Thomas Nassington (d. 1334), one of the most distinguished in this family of administrators, was described by Archbishop Grandisson as "vir utroque jure plurimum est instructus, in rebus agendis expertus, vite laudabilis, et pluribus allis articulis donis decoratus," a tribute given with just cause.[35] After his promotion to all orders in 1308, Thomas was granted a three-year license to study in 1320, and two-year licenses in 1323, 1324, and 1328. He studied in Bologna and returned to England. During this time, Thomas was appointed as official of Nottingham by Archbishop Grandisson. In 1318, at the petition of King Edward II, and Thomas, Earl of Lancaster, he received a papal appointment as rector of Yaxely in Huntingdon. Then in 1329 Grandisson made him official of the diocese of Exeter. He was given another papal provision in 1333 as ecclesiastical canon of York with the prebend of South Newbold. His final appointment as commissary of the ecclesiastical court of York brought his distinguished career as scholar, ecclesiastical lawyer, and dignitary of the church to a close.

Roger Nassington (d. 1364) served 47 years as canon and a civil-servant clerk.[36] His career began in 1321 when he received the title of <u>magister</u>, probably from Oxford. During his career, he received seven appointments as canon and prebend in Hereford, Wells, Beverley, and Lichfield. In 1322, he received the office of king's clerk, and soon he was granted protection while traveling overseas in the crown's service. His major appointment as chancellor of Lichfield was in 1329, a position he held until his death. The last year of his life he served as warden of St. Mary Magdalen Hospital in Southwell. Thus, as the detailed accounts of his activities in these offices show, Roger Nassington contributed almost a half-century of service to the English church.

All of the ecclesiastical and temporal records from the time of Archbishop John Romeyn in the late thirteenth century onward reveal the importance of these and even other Nassingtons.[37] Their high administrative offices, long tenures, appointments by church and state leaders indicate their competence and esteem. But they were not aloof from the pastoral needs of the English people, for as a result of the reform movement canons were generally obligated to reside in their prebends or cathedral churches and perform pastoral functions.[38]

Further evidence of the influence of the Nassingtons is the manor of Nassington, which supported a prebend for two and one-half centuries, indicating that the family were established landowners and churchmen. Le Neve's *Fasti* lists appointments for the Nassington prebend, beginning with John de Hawlyton in 1297, followed by 37 successive names to 1542,[39] including Roger Nassington as prebendary in 1318. The prebendal manor of Nassington began under Archbishop John Romeyn with a nonresident cleric but, as it flourished, it was given a cleric to support. The prebend of Nassington is identified as "the place of Nassington, Willybroof hundred, Northants, two and one-half miles southwest of Wansford, where the North Road crosses the Nene on its way north to Stamford."[40] According to Brown's introduction to the *Register of Archbishop Romeyn*, there is still a portion of the prebendal house there today.

William of Nassington: Priest and Poet

William of Nassington (d. 1359) served as chancellor of Exeter and official and vicar general of Durham at the time when these offices were most powerful, following the bishopric of John Thoresby (1352-1373), when the activities of bishops shifted from their diocese to the royal court.[41] However, his administration was not recorded with the same detail as that of the other

Nassingtons, for during this period the most important segment of the York register, the Officialitas Eborancenis, disappeared.[42] The eminent church historian, Robert Brentano, suggests that it is connected with the merger of the offices of official and vicar general.[43] As a consequence, the later part of William's life remains obscure.

However, confusion about William of Nassington arose from his association with the dioceses of Exeter and York, and sufficient research had not been done to gather the primary source material about his life. Furthermore, he had not been studied in the historical milieu of the fourteenth-century English church, which verified the common practice for bishops to appoint, simultaneously and successively, the same dignitaries or lawyers in more than one diocese. I have assembled an outline of the major events in the life of William of Nassington, taken primarily from the Registers of Archbishop Grandisson of Exeter and Archbishop Zouche of York, and from the Calendars of Patent and Close Rolls of Edward III. I have also discovered a transcription of his appointment by Zouche which proves that the William of Nassington who was appointed in York was the same individual as the William of Nassington who came from Exeter, thus resolving this crux.

    1328   Magister, probably of Oxford[44]

    1328   Portioner of Osmotherly, York[45]

    1328   Clerk of Bishop Grandisson, Nottingham[46]

1329 Canon and prebend of Bosham, Sussex[47]

1329 Proctor of the bishop at the Roman Curia[48]

1329 Rector of St. Phillack, Cornwall; clerk[49]

1329 Canon and prebend of Exeter; clerk[50]

1330 Rector of Bratton Clovelly, Devon[51]

1331 Rector of Newton, St. Cyres, Devon[52]

1331 Canon and prebend of Bosham by papal provision[53]

1331 Chancellor of Bishop Grandisson[54]

1332 Auditor of causes, Exeter[55]

1333 Rector of Morchard Bishop, Devon[56]

1333 Pardon for holding land without license, York[57]

1337 Executor of the will of Philip of Nassington[58]

1344 Canon of the king's free chapel in Hastings Castle and prebend of Malrepast[59]

1345 Chancellor of Archbishop Zouche, York[60]

1345 Visitation of Benedictine house of Weremouth, Durham[61]

1345 Vicar general sede vacante, Durham[62]

1345 Official sede vacante, Durham[63]

1345 Benefice as king's clerk, Chichester[64]

1346 Visitation to Lancaster[65]

1346 Auditor of causes, York[66]

1349 Canon and prebend of Bosham until death[67]

1349 Visitation to Carmelites at Denbigh, Lancaster[68]

1351 Proctor of clergy at Parliament, London[69]

1351   Prebend of Alton Australis, Salisbury[70]

1352   Resignation from benefice, Chichester[71]

1352   Made provision for the obituaries of Archbishop Grandisson and William de Meryet, chancellor Exeter[72]

1355   Official of Salisbury[73]

1359   Death; vacancy in the church of Bosham[74]

The earlier life of William of Nassington reflects the pattern of the other Nassington administrators. In 1328 he received the title <u>magister</u>, most likely from Oxford. That same year he began a succession of appointments as ecclesiastical lawyer and prebend in the dioceses of Sussex, Exeter, Devon, and York, with simultaneous appointments as rector, which involved him in active parish ministry. In 1331 Archbishop Grandisson appointed him as his chancellor at Exeter, an office that had expanded from the performance of secretarial duties to include visitations to religious houses as the archbishop's deputy. William flourished in Exeter as chancellor and ecclesiastical lawyer until 1345, when Archbishop William Zouche called him to be chancellor of York, an appointment transcribed in Zouche's Register as "...magistro Willelme de Nassington, canonico ecclesie cathedralis Exoniensis, clerico nostro familiari." This manuscript documents that the William of Nassington who was canon of Exeter was appointed at York, thus ending the errors claiming the existence of multiple figures with the same name. At York, he also conducted visitations to religious houses. Also in 1345 Zouche appointed him as vicar general and official of the vacant Durham see, granting him separate commissions for both offices to conduct visitations. In 1355 Zouche gave him yet another important ecclesiastical post as official to the Salisbury diocese.

In addition to these powerful offices in York and Exeter, William of Nassington seems to have been an astute master of both church and civil law, which was his primary occupation. In 1329 Archbishop Grandisson appointed him as his proctor to represent him at the Roman curia, although there are no records that he traveled to the papacy. However, William's name appears in the calendar of papal legislation because his appointment in 1331 as rector of Newton in Devon and to the canonry and prebend of Bosham were granted by papal provision at the petition of Archbishop Grandisson. In 1334 he was assigned as the lawyer of the king's free chapel in Hastings Castle. Following his move to York, he also served as one of the auditors of causes in the civil court and performed other civil services for King Edward III.

The official activities of archdiocesan lawyers are recorded in the pages of the registers.[75] The Register of John Grandisson documents William's involvement in approximately 80 cases, suggesting his broad knowledge of church law. One of his essential tasks at the diocesan courts was to write episcopal mandates, such as those arranging for the invocation of censures. He also upheld the right of the archbishop to conduct visitations, as, for example, in the dispute over his visitation at

Lancaster.[76] Much of his activity in the ecclesiastical court was taken up with drafting resolutions and legal procedures regarding benefices and their settlements. This often involved the disciplining of clergy regarding stipends and residency in order to enforce church reform. He also held jurisdiction over parochial boundaries, tithing, church rates, and prebendal payments. He had experience in dealing with all of the constituents of the fourteenth-century English church--episcopal administration, clergy, religious houses, and laity. With all of this experience, he most likely saw the need for reform, adequate clerical training, and spiritual instruction of the faithful. As an educated, committed cleric, William of Nassington, I contend, resolved to meet this need, and this brings me to his work as author and poet.

Primary evidence for the authorship of William of Nassington as a poet exists in two texts of the <u>Speculum Vitae</u>, MSS. B. L. Royal 17 C.viii, and B. L. Hatton 19:

>   Now wille I na mare say
>   ʒe haue herde, I ʒou pray,
>   þat ʒe wald pray specialy
>   For Freer John saule of Waldby,
>   þat fast studyd day and nyght
>   And made þis tale in Latyn right,
>   And preched it with fulle good chere
>   To lere and lewed þat hym wold here
>   þer Ihus Crist graunt hym mede
>   In hewyn for this good dede
>   Prays also with deuocioun
>   For Willm saule of Nassyngton,
>   þat gaf hym als fulle besyly
>   Night and day to grete study,
>   And made þis tale in ynglys tonge
>   Prays for hym old and ʒonge.[77]

This colophon is noted by Sir Frederick Madden in a footnote to Thomas Warton's History of English Poetry, II (1840). Warton concluded that, because the name of William of Nassington was associated with two separate works in different manuscripts, there were two Williams of Nassington, but he did not substantiate that conclusion:

> To this period belong two persons who had the same name in common, and who have been consequently confounded--two writers known as William of Nassyngton. One wrote a treatise De Trinitate et Unitate; the other, who was a proctor in the ecclesiastical court at York, translated into English John de Waldenby's Myrour of Life, of which there is a MS. dated 1418, in MS. Reg. 17 C.viii.[78]

Warton noted that the Myrour of Life had also been ascribed to Richard Rolle of Hampole in another manuscript, but that the text of the poem was the same as the one ascribed to Nassington.

In 1886, Carl Horstmann identified William of Nassington as a canon of York from the Thornton manuscript incipit to the Bande of Lovynge, an alternate title for the Tractatus de Trinitate et Unitate: "Incipit tractatus Willelmi Nassyngtone quondam advocati curiae Eboraci . . . ." Horstmann may have been following the citation in Perry's Religious Pieces (1887), which included the identical incipit and poem under its more common title. Horstmann based his primary identification on this incipit and, having stated that the Speculum Vitae and three other poems of MS. B. L. Cotton Tiberius C.VII were the work of the same author, William of Nassington, concluded with this assessment:

> So we have in him another Yorkshire poet of Richard
> Rolle's time, and his follower; but he is rather an
> easy versifier and translator, than an original thinker
> and poet.[79]

This erroneous and misleading biographical information on William of Nassington, which was given by Warton and Horstmann, was perpetuated by later critics. For example, A. F. Pollard in the <u>Dictionary of National Biography</u>, XIV (1885-), followed Warton in positing two Williams of Nassington and gave additional misinformation:

> Warton puts him as late as 1480; but as the transcript
> of his work in the Royal MSS is dated 1418, it is
> almost certain that he lived in the later half of the
> fourteenth century. He is probably distinct from the
> William of Nassyngton who is mentioned in connection
> with the church of St. Peter, Exeter (<u>in 1335 Cal. Inq.
> post</u> mortem, ii, 190b).[80]

In 1910, Hope Emily Allen, the perceptive scholar of Richard Rolle and other fourteenth-century mystics, examined the primary source material in the <u>Register of John Grandisson</u> and the Calendar of Patent and Close Rolls series for Edward III, and challenged the conclusions of these earlier critics:

> The poem <u>De Trinitate et Unitate</u>, here mentioned, occurs
> in the Thornton MS., where a note is found with it
> giving the information regarding William of Nassington's
> position as a proctor at York. This, our only piece of
> information regarding that person, is therefore connected
> with the first of Warton's two Williams of Nassington.[81]

Based upon a close study of Grandisson's register, Allen offered this important additional information on William:

> One, who was the chaplain of John de Grandisson, Bishop
> of Exeter, can be traced with considerable completeness
> from the accession of the bishop in 1326 to his own

> death in 1359. He was described in a letter to the Abbot of Wardon Abbey (perhaps fifty miles from Nassington in Northampton) as "orginaliter vobis non estraneus sed vicinus;" he was also said to be "utroque jure instructus." He held many benefices and, in the first years of his establishment at Exeter, he already held a benefice at Osmunderle in the diocese of York. It is the only one mentioned as belonging to him, in the letter to the abbot of Warden Abbey in 1328.[82]

Allen seems to favor the existence of a single person, but she could not reach a more definite conclusion.

The question of William of Nassington's identity arose again with Sir George F. Warner and Julius P. Gilson's 1921 publication of the _Catalog of Western Manuscripts in the Old Royal and King's Collections_, II. In describing MS. B. L. Royal 17 C.viii of the _Speculum Vitae_ and considering Nassington's authorship from the colophon and his identity from the Thornton incipit, they suggested that William of Nassington ". . . is perhaps the same as the chaplain (d. 1359) of John Grandisson, Bishop of Exeter," but they refuted the earlier claim about Waldeby as his source.[83] Thus, they implicitly challenged Horstmann's argument for two Williams of Nassington, and subscribed to Allen's findings.

In 1926 G. R. Owst, referring to Warner and Gilson's findings, opposed their suggestion that Archbishop John Grandisson's chaplain was the same William of Nassington who wrote the _Speculum Vitae_. Owst argued that Nassington's dates did not correspond with the dates of Waldeby (d. 1372) or with the colophon in MS. Bodleian 446, pointing out that in 1384 the _Speculum Vitae_ was examined at Cambridge for heresy for four days but declared sound and orthodox.[84] Because Owst presumed that Waldeby was the source for Nassington, and that Nassington lived at the time the Speculum Vitae was certified, he concluded that the Speculum Vitae was written in 1384. He was in error in all of these accounts, for in 1917 Allen established that 1) Waldeby wrote no such tract as Nassington attributed to Waldeby, 2) Nassington died in 1359, and 3) his work was certified in 1384.

Other discussions of William of Nassington and the Speculum Vitae have continued these erroneous opinions. In 1928 Frances Comper[85] reiterated Horstmann's conclusions regarding two Williams of Nassington, and in 1969 Agnes David Gunn added to the confusion by expanding the list to six:

> More than one man of this name lived in the fourteenth century, indeed, six are listed in contemporary records apart from quondam advocati curie Eboraci, an ecclesiastical lawyer at York mentioned in the Thornton manuscript.[86]

Although Gunn relied on Allen's resources, even to the reproduction of a typographical error in one of the documentations cited from the patent and close rolls series, she misinterpreted Allen's findings, and presumed that each individual entry in the records referred to a separate person.

The critical confusion concerning the identity of William of Nassington and his activity in both Exeter and York is clarified by my research, in which I continue the direction suggested by Allen and document his biography through nearly one hundred entries from primary sources. William of Nassington was not only an ecclesiastical lawyer who earned the respect of the English church and state, but also a poet whose extensive work has largely been overlooked. The church reform calling for instruction of the clergy and laity, the renown of his family, and his ecclesiastical accomplishments culminate in the <u>Speculum Vitae</u>. This remarkable work and the minor works ascribed to William of Nassington--the <u>Tractatus de Trinitate et Unitate</u>, <u>St. Mary's Lamentation to St. Bernard on the Passion of Christ</u>, <u>Form of Living</u> in verse, <u>Spiritus Guydonis</u>, and the Northern Homily collection--will be discussed in the following chapters.

NOTES

[1] Wilkins, D. ed., <u>Concilia Britanniae et Hiberniae</u>, I (London, 1737).

[2] C. R. Cheney, <u>English Synodalia of the Thirteenth Century</u>, (Oxford: University Press, 1941), pp. 16-53, traces the relationship of the councils to the synods as summarized in the following paragraphs. General accounts of the English synods are given in M. Gibbs and J. Lang, <u>Bishops and Reform, 1215-1271</u> (Oxford, 1934); E. J. Arnould, ed., <u>Le Manuel des Peches</u> (Paris, 1940).

[3] Cheney, 8-9. Canon was the recognized word for the general acts of a papal council, which I will use to distinguish between the refinements legislated by the provincial councils and diocesan synods.

[4] S. H. Thomson, <u>The Writings of Robert Grosseteste</u> (Cambridge: University Press, 1940), p. 138, assesses the importance of the Constitutions.

[5] Wilkins, II, trans. Sr. Dympna Skelley (n.p., n.p., 1982).

[6] G. H. Russell, "Vernacular Instruction of the Laity in the Later Middle Ages in England: Some Texts and Notes," <u>Journal of Religious History</u>, 2 (1962), pp. 98-99, credits this point to L. E. Boyle in the "<u>Oculus Sacerdotis</u> and Some Other Works of William Pagula," <u>Trans. Royal Historical Society</u>, 5th Series, (1955), p. 82.

[7] Helen P. Forshaw, ed., <u>Edmund of Abington: Speculum Religiosorum and Speculum Ecclesie</u> (London: Oxford University Press, 1973); and Harry Wolcott Robbins, ed., <u>Saint Edmund's "Merure de Seinte Eglise" An Early Example of Rhythmical Prose</u> (Lewisburg, Pa: University Print Shop, 1923). Allan Wilshire, "The Latin Primacy of St. Edmund's 'Mirror of Holy Church' " <u>Modern Language Review</u>, 71 (1976), 500-12, argues that the original work is the Latin version.

[8]See the section, "Extant Texts and Their Editing," pp. 217-24, in C. R. Cheney, "Legislation of the Medieval English Church. Part I," The English Historical Review, 198 (1935), p. 193-224 for a full treatment of the copying and resultant discrepancies in ecclesiastical texts. Cheney estimates that for each set of provincial canons belonging to the period 1222-1342, there were, on the average, some fifty texts available.

[9]W. A. Pantin, The English Church in the Fourteenth Century (Cambridge: University Press, 1955), p. 194.

[10]See Aubrey Gwynn, The English Friars in the Time of Wyclif (London, 1940), pp. 114-23.

[11]Pantin, "The Legacy of the Thirteenth Century," pp. 1-5.

[12]Pantin, "The Social Structure of the English Church," pp. 9-11.

[13]Waldo Smith, "Appointments to English Sees, 1307-27," Episcopal Appointments and Patronage in the Reign of Edward II (Chicago: American Society of Church History, 1938), p. 11.

[14]For other general discussions see Paul Fournier's Les Officialites au Moyen Age (Paris: E. Plon, 1880); A. Hamilton Thompson, The English Clergy and Their Organization in the Later Middle Ages (Oxford: Clarendon Press, 1947); and Christopher R. Cheney, English Bishops' Chanceries 1100-1250 (Manchester: Manchester University Press, 1950).

[15]Robert Brentano, "Late Medieval Changes in the Administration of Vacant Suffragan Dioceses: Province of York," Yorkshire Archeological Journal, 38 (1955), p. 496-503.

[16]John Moorman, "Chapels, Chantries and Collegiate Churches," Church life in England in the Thirteenth Century. (Cambridge: University Press, 1955), pp. 18-19. See A. H. Thompson, The Cathedral Churches of England (New York: Macmillan, 1925), p. 211.

[17] Moorman, "The Parishes of England," p. 4, estimates this number as a median between 8025 parishes listed on the Taxio Nicholai list of 1291 counted by Cutts, Parish Priests and Their People, p. 385; and the 12,280 parishes claimed by A. R. Powys, The English Parish Church, pp. xv, 19. Moorman estimates that Lincoln and York each had about forty and Exeter about twenty. See Pantin's "The Parish Clergy," pp. 27-29, for an expansion of this discussion on the appointment and education of the parish clergy.

[18] Edward Peacock, ed., Instructions for Parish Priests by John Myrk, EETS, OS 31, 1868, 1. Myrk's verse treatise is an adaptation of a Latin original, the second part of the Oculus Sacerdotis (1330), ascribed to William of Pagula (d. 1332), for the use of the unlearned clergy.

[19] Moorman, pp. 5-6, turns to G. Barraclough, Papal Provisions, p. 54, "The essentially material interests of the aristocratic classes make it normal to regard the religious vocation from the standpoint not of officium, but of beneficium."

[20] Pantin, p. 29.

[21] A. Hamilton Thompson, The English Clergy and Their Organization in the Later Middle Ages. (Oxford: Clarendon Press, 1947), p. 48. When the archbishop was absent and episcopal acts were necessary (ordinations, confirmations, consecrations of chapels and churchyards, reconciliation of consecrated sites polluted by bloodshed, benediction of heads of religious houses, the consecration of the holy oil and chrism on Holy Thursday), the services of a suffragan were called in. From the early part of the fourteenth century, the employment of a suffragan became fairly common.

[22] Thompson, p. 22, elaborates upon these and other duties of the vicar general.

[23] Thompson, "The Registers of the Archbishops of York," The Yorkshire Archeological Journal, 32 (1936), 249. The surviving English registers come from Archbishops Walter Grey (1215-55) and Romeyn of York. Other registers survive from the archbishops of Canterbury, Bath, Wells, Coventry, Litchfield, Exeter, Hereford Norwich, Salisbury, Winchester, and Carlisle.

[24] Surtees Society Publications include the Register of John Romeyn and Henry Newark, Archbishops of York 1288-96, 1296-99, ed. W. Brown, I, 123, II 128; Register of William of Greenfield, Archbishop of York 1306-1315, eds. W. Brown and A. H. Thompson, I, 145, II, 149, III, 151, IV, 152, V, 153; and the Register of Thomas Corbridge, Archbishop of York 1300-1304, eds. W. Brown and A. H. Thompson, I, 138, II, 141. Available in manuscript are: the Register of Archbishop Melton, Archbishop of York, 1317-1340, and the Register of William Zouche, Archbishop of York, 1342-1352. Other major ecclesiastical records of the Nassington family are in John Le Neve, Fasti Ecclesiae Anglicanae 1300-1541, 12 vols. (University of London; Institute of Historical Research, rpt., Athlone Press, 1962-67), and the Calendar of Papal Legislation, the Calendar of Patent Rolls, and the Calendar of Close Rolls in A. B. Emden., ed., A Biographical Register of the University of Oxford to A. D. 1500, II (Oxford: Clarendon Press, 1958), pp. 1337-39.

[25] Emden, A. D., ed., A Biographical Register of the University of Oxford to A. D. 1500, II (Oxford: Clarendon Press, 1958), 1337-38; Reg. Greenfield, 153, 96.

[26] Reg. Greenfield, 153, 96.

[27] Reg. Greenfield, 145, 128.

[28] C.P.R., 1301-07; Reg. Greenfield, 145, 36, 46, 47-48, 50, 64, 72-73, 75, 78, 80, 87, 105, 113, 294; Reg. Corbridge, 138, 24, 44, 72-74, 127.

[29] C.P.R., 1313-17, 631.

[30] Emden, II, pp. 1337-38. See Reg. Greenfield, 153, lii-liii, on the difficulty in the records distinguishing the Johns of Nassington. The third John, magister, junior advocate on the court of York in 1314, Reg. Greenfield, 145, 153; auditor of causes of dean and chapter of York in 1306, still in 1310, Reg. Greenfield, 149, 151, 58; official of York in 1316, Reg. Greenfield, 153, liii, 245, 252, 255, 256, 258, 277, 282.

[31] Reg. Greenfield, 154, 130, n.; Emden, II, 1337. Emden notes a dispensation on account of illegitimacy for promotion to orders granted to John, Junior, in 1308, and for Thomas in 1308.

[32] Emden, II, 1338.

[33] Le Neve, III, 154.

[34] Reg. Melton, fol. 472v, in Brentano, 500, transcribed 501-02.

[35] Emden, II, 1338-39.

[36] Emden, II, 1338.

[37] Phillip Nassington, apparently not a magister, appears in the Reg. Grandisson, III, in 1330 as clerk at Clyst (#1278), in 1334 as priest of Clyst (#1307), in 1349 installed at Farnum (#1381), and in 1363 in Winchester (#1491). Other Nassingtons are: Henry, 1298, prebend of Grantham Australis, Salisbury (LeNeve, III, 53); Hugh, 1308, dispensed as clerk of York (Reg. Greenfield, 153, 289); Nicholas, Extracts from the Account Rolls of the Abbey of Durham, II, SS, 100, 510.

[38] Thompson, The English Clergy, points out that the distinction by which residents are called canons, and non-residents prebendaries is comparatively modern. He gives Lynwood's definition of a prebend, which is the consequence of a canonry. Provisions to canonries with the expectations of prebends were frequent, but it was not until they acquired prebends that they became full members of a chapter, p. 77, n.1.

[39] Le Neve, I, "Prebendaries of Nassington," 94-96. The entry in Le Neve for John Lascy, who was given a royal grant on November 21, 1299, by reason of vacancy, suggests its independence may have been earlier than this record. John Dronkensford, who was to become archbishop, was Lascy's successor. He was appointed when the king complained that the bishop had taken no action on the vacancy in Nassington. Archbishop Romeyn had been prebend of Nassington before his appointment to York. Following him, there was a long litigation for the possession of Nassington between the crown and bishops of Lincoln which was not ended until the reign of Edward III. Reg. Romeyn, 123, 338, notes that Nassington appears as prebend on March 19, 1287-88, where the authority of Gaudin de Aseby to collect the first fruits as "privilegialiter pertinentes" and the fourth part of the benefices of the non-resident is on record.

[40] Reg. Romeyn, 123, 26.

[41] Brentano, 489. With the more frequent absence of the bishop, the role of the chancellor expanded. Chaney traces this from the time of Romeyn to William of Nassington, and provides the sources to illustrate the evolving role of chancellor, p. 42, n. 2; Reg. Romeyn and Newark, 123, 35, 40n, 171; Reg. Greenfield, 152, 69; Reg. Greenfield, 145, 24. See also Irene Churchill, Quarterly Administration, I (1933), pp. 25-35.

[42] Thompson, "The Registers of the Archbishops of York," The Yorkshire Archeological Journal, 32 (1936), 253. Under Archbishop Greenfield, the two offices of vicar general and official were sometimes connected through the person holding them, but this was not the usual pattern. In studying the section of the Register of William Zouche which relates to the archdeaconry of Richmond, Thompson observes that the "archiepiscopal registers include no continuous series of documents which bear upon its ecclesiastical history; and it was only during periods in which the office of archdeacon was vacant that much of its business came immediately before the archbishop and his clerks." Also see Thompson, "Some Letters From the Register of William Zouche, Archbishop of York," p. 327.

[43] Brentano, 500-01. Brentano discovers, however, in connection with Nassington's appointments, "a peculiar subtlety with which the new superior official, the vicar general, was inserted into the vacant hierarchy."99

[44] Emden, II, 1339.

[45] Portioner of Osmotherly, still in 1331. Reg. Grandisson, I, 167-68.

[46] Reg. Grandisson, II, 662, in Emden, 1339.

[47] Reg. Grandisson, III, 1265. The collegiate Church of Bosham. Master William de Nassyngtone, clerk, was collated (at Chudleigh) 4 Sept. to his canonry and prebend (we are not told which of the prebends). Letters of induction were directed to the sacristan on the same day. Many entries in the registers begin like this one, with a place named after the date, which appears to be where the archbishop was traveling at the time.

[48] Reg. Grandisson, I, 476, in Emden, I.

[49] Reg. Grandisson, III, 1269. Master William de Nassyngtone, clerk, was collated by lapse (at Clyst), 8 March. Mandate for induction direction to the Archdeacon of Cornwall and to Richard de Gomersale, Rector of Dittisham.

[50] Reg. Grandisson, III, 1274. Master William de Nassyngtone, clerk, was collated (at Chudleigh) 24 October, 1330.

[51] Reg. Grandisson, III, 1279. Bratton Clovely, Archdeaconry of Exeter. On the resignation of Master Robert Broke, Master William de Nassyngtone, Canon of Exeter, was installed (at Clyst) 1 July. Patrons, the Prior and Convent of Plympton; administered July 1, 1330, exchanged Feb. 1333. Reg. Grandisson, III, 1291.

[52] C. Pap. L., II, 362, in Emden, II, 1339.

[53] Was granted canonry and prebend of Bosham by papal provision at the petition of Bishop Grandisson, even though he already was canon and prebend of Exeter, portion of Osmotherly, and rectory of Newton St. Cyres. Dec., 17, 1331. C. Pap. R. II, 362, in Emden, II, 1339.

[54] Reg. Grandisson, III, 1714, still chancellor of the bishop in 1334.

[55] Reg. Zouche, fol. 268v, in Emden, 1339. Collated Feb. 9.

[56] Reg. Grandisson, III, 1292.

[57] C. P. R., 1332, 383. Jan. 22. Pardon to William de Nassyngton for acquiring in fee from Alice late the wife of John le Leche of Clyve 48 acres 3 roods of land in Haryshagh and Caluhey in Clyve forest, said to be held in chief and entering thereon without license, and license for him to retain the same. By fine of 10s. Northampton.

[58] C. P. R., 1336-1337, 736. The Tower. Jan. 16. William de Nassyngton and William de Stauford, executor of the will of Master Philip de Nassyngtone, put in their place William de Welyngoure, clerk, to prosecute the execution of a recognizance for 20 marks made to Philip in chancery by John Haye, son and heir of Richard Haye and by John le Forester of Hagton.

[59] C. P. R., 1336-1227. Nov. 6, Melford. Presentation of Master William de Nassyngton to the prebend of Malrepost in the king's free chapel of Hastynges, in the diocese of Chicester, void by the resignation of William de Feriby, admitted by R. bishop of Chichester; 9 Edward III, 477. June 7. Westminster. Mandate to the dean and chapter of the king's free chapel of Hastynges to assign to Master William de Nassyngton, King's clerk, a stall in the choir and a place in the chapter in right of the prebend of Malrepost in their chapel, to which prebend, void by the resignation of William de Feriby, admitted by R., bishop of Rochester.

[60] The Inventories and Account Rolls of the Benedictine Houses or Cells. Jarrow and Monk-Wearmouth in the County of Durham, SS, 29,47.

[61] Reg. Zouche, fol. 282v, in Brentano, 500; transcribed p. 502. Zouche commissioned William of Nassington his vicar general in the vacant see of Durham 15 April 1335.

[62] Reg. Zouche, fol. 283, in Brentano, 500; transcribed, p. 502. On 24 April, Zouche commissioned the same William Nassington, a canon of Exeter and Zouche's clerk and familiar, official of the vacant see.

[63] Reg. Melton, fol. 472; Reg. Zouche, fol. 283, in Brentano 500. In both cases additional commissions were given for visitations.

[64] Canon of the king's free chapel in Hastings Castle and prebendary of Malrepost. Vacant by December 1352. C. P. R., 1343-45, 374-396, in Emden, II, 1339.

[65] Reg. Zouche, fol. 68, related in Thompson, "Some Letters from the Register of William Zouche, Archbishop of York," pp. 328-29. This was the primary visitation by Zouche to his archdeaconry. No program of the visitation, such as it was customary to record for the registers, remains; but it was apparently delayed until the Lent of 1346, and was then entrusted to commissaries, the chief of whom was the archbishop's chancellor, William of Nassington. On their way to hold their visitation at Lancaster, the commissaries found their road beset by ambushes of armed men from the neighborhood. The messenger whom they sent to treat with these insurgents was seized and imprisoned, together with the rural dean of Amounderness, who had shown respect to the visitors. The keys of the priory of Lancaster, which had been prepared for the reception of the commissaries, were violently taken from the prior and his servants, the gates and doors were barred, and the provisions laid in for the occasion were consumed. No grounds for this outbreak are stated, and it may have been a mere act of lawlessness, like the riot which took place in Southwell Minster on Whitsunday, 1348, when an attempt was made by some 'satellites of Satan' to carry off the obligations of the faithful (ff 228, 228v). The hard treatment received by the rural dean, however, whose fault was that he had received the commissaries with due reverence, indicates that the opposition was directed against the archbishop's right to visit an exempt jurisdiction with which his predecessors had interfered only at rare intervals.

[66] Appointed April 10, 1336. Reg. Zouche, fol. 268v, in Emden, II, 1339.

[67] Reg. Grandisson, III, 1376, 1452, Bosham. Master William de Nassyngton was collated (at Chudleigh) to the prebend of Westbroke, March 2.

[68] Reg. Zouche, fol. 268v, 270, reported by Thompson, "Some Letters from the Register of William Zouche, Archbishop of York," pp. 328-29. Nassington conducts a visitation in behalf of Zouche as protector of the order of friars in England and Wales. From the accompanying documents it is practically certain that it was 1349-50 when the Bishop of Asaph exceeded his authority by presuming to excommunicate the prior of the Carmelites at Denbigh without respecting the exemption from episcopal jurisdiction enjoyed by the order, and had disregarded the prior's petition for the removal of the sentence. Appeal was made to Zouche as conservator and judge of the order, who accordingly took action to warn the bishop. The sequel of such admonitions is so often left unrecorded that it is satisfactory to find from the second letter that, after some interval, the bishop was persuaded to change his attitude and that the incident apparently ended peacefully in the summer of 1351.

[69]"Dewsbury Account Rolls," *The Yorkshire Archeological Journal*, 23 (1911), 381. For the expense of Master William de Nassyngton, official of Pontefract, proctor of the clergy in York diocese, riding to London to Parliament for the York clergy.

[70]Le Neve, III, 21. Prebendaries of Alton Australis in Salisbury Diocese, installed 31 May (Corffe, AC, p. 69).

[71]*C. P. R.*, 1352, 396, Jan. 28. Westminster. Mandate to the dean and chapter of the king's free chapel of Hastynges to assign a stall in the choir and a place in the chapter of Philip de Nassyngton, who, on the king's presentation, had been instituted by R., Bishop of Chichester, to the prebend of Marlepas in the said chapel, void by the resignation of Master William de Nassyton.

[72]*C. P. R.*, 1354-58, p. 91, in Emden, II, 1339.

[73]*Cal. Arch. Queen's Coll.*, IV, 529, in Emden, II, 1339.

[74]*Reg. Grandisson*, III, 1452. Bosham. On the death of Master William de Nassington, Sir Thomas Kaignes, priest, was collated (at Chudleigh) to the Prebend of Westbroke, June 17.

[75]Dorothy M. Owen, ed., *John Lydford's Book* (London: HMSO, 1974), discusses the difficulty of interpreting the professional duties of clerks and ecclesiastical canons from the registers. Some of this information is adapted from her introduction, especially pages 15-18, where she is able to draw conclusions about church courts and administrations from her preparation of John Lydford's memorandum book. In addition to the scholarship on this topic by Pantin, L. E. Boyle, G. Barraclough, and T. F. Tout, which I have cited in the notes for this chapter, Owen suggests the work of K. L. Wood-Legh, *Studies in Church Life in England under Edward III*, (Cambridge, 1934).

[76]The process by which the archbishop came to make visitations is traced by James Raine, *Historians of the Church of York*, Rolls Series, II, pp. 148-49.

[77]John W. Smeltz, ed., "*Speculum Vitae*: An Edition of British Museum Manuscript Royal, 17, C, VIII," Diss. Dusquesne University, 1977, pp. 713-14.

[78] Thomas Warton, History of English Poetry from the Twelfth to the Close of the Sixteenth Century, II, ed., W. Hazlitt (London: Reeves and Turner, 1871, rpt., Hildesheim: Georg Olms Verlagsbuchhandlung, 1968), p. 116.

[79] Horstmann, Yorkshire Writers, II, 274.

[80] Oxford: Oxford University Press, 120.

[81] "The Authorship of the Prick of Conscience," Studies in English and Comparative Literature (Boston: Ginn, 1910), p. 167.

[82] Reg. Grandisson, I, 168, in Allen, p. 167, n.2.

[83] Warner and Gilson, p. 240.

[84] G. R. Owst, Preaching in Medieval England (Cambridge: University Press, 1926), p. 289.

[85] Frances Comper, The Life of Richard Rolle together with an Edition of his English Lyrics (New York: E. P. Dutton, 1928).

[86] "Accidia and Prowess in the Vernon Version of Nassyngton's Speculum Vitae," Diss. University of Pennsylvania, 1969, p. 6.

CHAPTER II

AUTHORSHIP, DATE, AND PROVENANCE OF THE SPECULUM VITAE

William of Nassington's authorship of the Speculum Vitae rests on two ascriptions found in the texts contained in MSS. B. L. Royal 17 C. viii and Hatton 19, and his authorship of the Tractatus de Trinitate et Unitate on the incipit in the Thornton manuscript. Yet the question of Nassington's authorship has been highly controversial. The problem is further complicated by the scholarly confusion over the dates of the manuscripts, texts of the Speculum Vitae and the Tractatus de Trinitate et Unitate, and their sources, especially the relationship of Nassington and John Waldeby. Resolving these questions of authorship, manuscript dates, and sources provides the context to study the Speculum Vitae.

In addition, the poem must be considered in its generic and theological dimensions. Three medieval religious genres inform the Speculum Vitae: the summa, the speculum primarily concerned with the vices and virtues, and the Pater Noster tract with its schema of seven petitions. These instructional and devotional texts were in the mainstream of moral and ascetical theology, which had its foundation in the patristic writers, continued into the Middle Ages, and culminated in works such as William of Nassington's 16,396-line compilation, the Speculum Vitae.

Authorship of the Speculum Vitae

The colophon naming William of Nassington as author of the Speculum Vitae from MS. B. L. Royal C. viii, included at the end of Chapter I of my study, was printed by Madden in Warton's 1840 History of English Poetry, II.[1] With this notice Warton initiated, not only the error about two Williams of Nassington, but a second series of errors about his texts and their sources. In 1885 A. F. Pollard confused the text of the Speculum Vitae with the Tractatus de Trinitate et Unitate, attributing the Speculum Vitae to Richard Rolle, and giving John Waldeby as a source for the Tractatus. In 1907, The Cambridge History of English Literature iterated Pollard's errors. In 1910 Hope Emily Allen began to untangle these inaccuracies by correctly identifying the texts of the Speculum Vitae and the Tractatus de Trinitate et Unitate, and giving the manuscript evidence that associates Waldeby with the Speculum Vitae, but not with the Tractatus:

> Halliwell (Thornton Romances, p. xxx) notes of it: "Warton has confused this poem, which has no merit, with Nassington's translation of Waldeby. The mistake was corrected by Sir F. Madden in Warton's History (II. 368), where the commencing lines do not seem to be accurately given." Mr. A. F. Pollard, in the Dict. of Nat. Biog., entirely confuses this poem with the Speculum Vitae. He declares that "Nassington's one claim to remembrance is his translation into English verse of the Treatise on the Trinity and Unity . . . written in Latin by one John de Waldeby . . . . The Myrour of Life, sometimes attributed to Richard Rolle, is identical with Nassington's translation." The compiler of the bibliography for the Camb. Hist. Eng. Lit. also (II, 498), implies that the shorter poem of Nassington is likewise from John de Waldeby. He

states that 'Nassington translated some Latin works, such as one of Waldeby's <u>On the Trinity and Unity</u>, and also his <u>Myrour of Life</u>.[2]

The question of Nassington's authorship was further complicated by false attributions of the <u>Speculum Vitae</u> to Richard Rokeby and Richard Rolle. Casley's <u>Catalogue</u> incorrectly assigned the authorship of the poem to Richard Rokeby, who was named as the transcriber of the poem in MS. B. L. Royal 17 C. viii:

> þat ȝe may come ȝe hyns wend
> To the blys with outyn ende,
> To whilk blys he us brynge.
> þat on þe crosse for us wold hynge.
> Amen quod Rycerdus Rokeby.
>   ora pro me, frater.[3]

In 1802 Joseph Ritson corrected Casley's error,[4] and subsequently the Warner and Gilson <u>Catalog of Royal Manuscripts</u> affirmed Ritson's emendation based on Rokeby's signature in the Royal manuscript.

The attribution of the <u>Speculum Vitae</u> to Richard Rolle is understandable because of Rolle's popularity in the fourteenth century and the frequency with which devotional works were assigned to him. In her account of false ascriptions to Rolle, Allen quotes the attribution of the <u>Speculum Vitae</u> to Rolle in MS. Cambridge Ll. 1, 8, of the late fourteenth century:

> Explicit quidam tractatus super pater noster secundum Ricardum Hampolem qui obit Anno domini millesimo ccc^{mo} octogesimo quarto. Reynoldus cognomen scriptoris possidet amen.[5]

Allen notes that the <u>Speculum Vitae</u> follows Rolle's <u>Meditations on the Passion</u> and imputes the false attribution to a careless scribe who may have copied the same verse tag for both works.

The most adamant proponent of Richard Rolle as author of the Speculum Vitae was J. Ullmann in 1884. He based his argument on the first 370 lines of the Speculum Vitae text from Cambridge University Ll, 1, 8, with its attribution to Rolle.[6] Furthermore, he made elaborate comparisons between the style of the Speculum Vitae and the Prick of Conscience, arguing that they were both the work of Richard Rolle. Ullmann denied the reliability of the attribution to Nassington, claiming that two ascriptions were not sufficient manuscript evidence to establish authorship.

In 1910 and 1917 Hope Emily Allen refuted Ullmann and others. She showed that Ullmann's stylistic comparisons did not disprove Rolle as the author of the Prick of Conscience. Rather, Allen contended that Ullmann's argument could be used with equal validity to claim that Nassington was the author of both poems:

> Any attempt to settle the question of the authorship of the Speculum Vitae is at present blocked by our ignorance of everything connected with the traditional author of the poem. But the character of advocate at an ecclesiastical court, given him by our only information, is such as would be far more suitable to the author of the Prick of Conscience--and apparently of the Speculum Vitae--than would be that of an original and devoted mystic, like the hermit of Hampole.[7]

Seven years later, Allen accused Ullmann of plagiarizing his classifications of style from dissertations analyzing Old French writers, again charging that the norms he used to test the authorship of both poems were invalid.[8] Allen examined 31 manuscripts of the Speculum Vitae, and noted that the attributions in MSS. Royal 17 C. viii and Hatton 19 naming Nassington were substantially the same.[9] She pointed out that nine of the manuscripts were incomplete at the end, where an authorial ascription would ordinarily be found.[10] In this 1917 updating of her 1910 monograph, Allen commented again on the problem of Nassington and the authorship of the Speculum Vitae:

> It must be said at once that the examination of the manuscripts of the Speculum has increased the uncertainty as to its authorship. The name of William of Nassington has not been found attached to more than two copies already known, and no name of another author has been substituted. Nothing has been added to our information as to this person, and he may or may not be the author of the Speculum.[11]

In 1927 Allen in Writings Ascribed to Richard Rolle rejected Rolle and pointed to Nassington as the likely author:

> It gives no hint of Rolle, and is--on a large scale--a work alien to his writings. William of Nassington, on the other hand, is a person to whom it could be plausibly attributed. He was, apparently, a resident of York (an advocate at the archiepiscopal court), and another work is ascribed to him sufficiently like the Speculum in style and sentiment. The manuscript evidence for his authorship is stronger than for Rolle's, not only because it occurs in two copies against Rolle's one, but also because it occurs in the text, whereas the attribution to Rolle is given in a verse tag by a scribe . . . .[12]

Although more than 50 years have elapsed since Allen's critical studies, no significant new evidence has been forthcoming on the authorship of the Speculum Vitae. The two manuscript ascriptions continue to be the most significant evidence to establish Nassington as poet. In his 1953 survey of theological writings in medieval England, A. I. Doyle reached the same tentative decision about Nassington as Allen:

> From an interpolation found only in a couple of copies, of doubtful authority, but likely enough, he is supposed to have been William of Nassington, the author of the Bande of Lovyng mentioned earlier (pt. I, sec 2b), a secular priest and ecclesiastical lawyer in the archiepiscopal court of York and other dioceses, like the author of the Manuel des Peches a century before; one by experience well aware of the field and able to employ wide theoretical and practical knowledge cultivating it in the most effective way, having no doubt also, in his position, every encouragement and facility to disseminate his work as broadly and speedily as possible.[13]

Following Allen and Doyle, Saara Nevanlinna in her 1976 edition of the Northern Homily Cycle commented on the unascribed Speculum Vitae in MS. Cotton Tiberius E. VII:

> It is not impossible that the lines about Nassyngton's authorship were left out by the reviser on purpose. It was not customary for a composer of religious poetry to disclose his identity.[14]

Although he was an important ecclesiastical figure, William of Nassington did not enjoy the widespread popularity of Rolle, whose fame as a mystic brought innumerable erroneous ascriptions to him. Accordingly, the attributions authenticating Nassington to be the poet of the Speculum Vitae, found in MSS. B. L. Royal 17 C. viii and Hatton 19 cannot and should not be discounted.

In addition, the biographical information about Nassington not known by Allen, and now provided in my Chapter I, corroborates the historical ambience, ecclesiastical training, knowledge of church and state law, acquaintance with different classes of English society, and involvement with reform legislation which are reflected in this compendium. Therefore, I hold that William of Nassington is the author of the Speculum Vitae.

As a magister, experienced in church and state law, Nassington was prepared to compile a document illustrating the basic dogma which was mandated for church membership. As a devout churchman who knew the pastoral needs of the faithful, he also was able to provide a guide to prayer and perfection based on the via mystica. The author of the Speculum Vitae accomplishes this two-fold purpose, using its doctrinal foundation for a treatise on perfection. The Speculum Vitae responds to the didactic needs of the reform movement and to the devotional needs of increasing numbers of educated laity and religious who hungered for personal union with God in prayer.

The poet of the Speculum Vitae is one versed in scripture, the church fathers, and papal and English legislation. Nassington's intellectual range is evident in his commentaries and illustrations, such as the discussions of the vices and virtues with their branches and roots. As a corollary to his scholarship, Nassington's service as a canon and cleric provided him with contemporary exempla from a variety of social levels. With gentle wit, he chides the noble ladies, who come to church with their silver, pearls, and precious stones, about the deceit of riches (10,887-10,892), and the slothful who lie in bed loving their ease when they should be attending mass (5051-5064). His discussions include reminders of ecclesiastical regulations, such as those governing proper transfer of a benefice (1779-1798), to denouncements, for example, that of the uncontrolled anger of the householder who, like a crazy man, throws pots and cups (4665-4676).

While the commentaries in Speculum Vitae mirror Nassington's life as a canonist and administrator, they unfold the richness of his interior life as a scholar and mystic. Nassington is dedicated to the institutional church, grieved by its human imperfections, zealous for reform, and fearless in declaring abuse; consequently, he urges its members to contrition and amendment. Yet Nassington describes the human ignorance and weakness of the church with tender devotion, explaining how sin incites the merciful forgiveness of the Father, the redemptive suffering and death of God the Son, and the invitation for salvation and perfection through the grace of the Holy Spirit. Nassington's heart is moved as he recounts the universality of this call to perfection. He exclaims with prayerful gratitude that although human nature could not merit its elevation to a supernatural state, God the Father calls all persons of faith to become his adopted sons, to participate in the eternal inheritance, to respond to the prompting of grace through the new law of the Beatitudes. Through the petitions of the Pater Noster, Nassington instructs his audience in the way of perfection, fulfilled in mystical union.

Manuscript Dates and Circulation

Errors in dating the Speculum Vitae manuscripts began with Horstmann in 1886, who gave 1350 as the date of MS. B. L. Cotton

Tiberius E. VII.[15] Later authorities have shown this date to be inaccurate. In 1883 H. L. D. Ward's Catalog of Romances in the British Musuem placed this manuscript circa 1400, which agrees with Ullmann, Wells, Brown and Robbins, and Venetia Nelson.[16] Three manuscripts establish 1384 as the terminus ad quem for the Speculum Vitae: Cambridge I1. i., Bodleian 445, and Caius College 160:

> In the year of Our Lord 1384, this compilation was examined at Cambridge in this manner. While it was left there by a certain priest, in order to be bound, it was carefully looked at by certain scholars, and read through and presented to the Chancellor of the University and his Council, in order to be examined for defects and heresies; lest the unlearned should carelessly deceive the people through its means, and fallaciously lead them into various errors. Then by command of the Chancellor, before him and the whole Council of the University, it was examined for four days with all care and diligence, and tested in every college on every side; and on the fifth day all the doctors of both laws and the masters of theology, together with the Chancellor, declared and affirmed that it was well and subtly drawn out of the sacred laws and divine books, and that it was alleged, affirmed and founded on the authority of all the Doctors of the Sacred Page. Therefore, whoever you are, O reader, do not despise this work, because without a doubt, if any defects had been found in it, it would have been burnt before the University of Cambridge.[17]

Such examinations of religious writings for orthodoxy became mandatory in England as a result of the widespread heretical Lollard movement headed by John Wycliffe. Allen reports that by 1408, the suspicion of Lollardy was so great that by order of the Constitutions of Archbishop Arundel, "all books written in the time of John Wycliffe or since, were subject to examination."[18]

Since Lollardy was flourishing by the time of Wycliffe's death in 1384, and Nassington's work was examined that year, it would seem likely that the endorsement of the Speculum Vitae affirmed an already-popular text.[19] John de Burgh, who was appointed Chancellor of the University of Cambridge in 1384,[20] probably examined and approved the Speculum Vitae, and in the following year issued his Pupilla oculi, a similar extensive compilation of doctrine and devotion. The rapidity with which the Speculum Vitae was approved as an orthodox manual of spiritual instruction also suggests a prior popularity.

In this connection, because of the 1384 sanction of the Cambridge ecclesiastics, A. I. Doyle thinks that the poem had circulated significantly before that date, a conclusion verified by his meticulous study of the dissemination of religious writings in the Middle Ages. Doyle traces the audience of the manuscripts of the Speculum Vitae, and reports on the two fifteenth-century manuscripts crucial to this study--Hatton 19 and Royal 17 C. viii:

> Hatton 19 belonged to a monastery, and Royal 17, c, viii, was apparently written for another community probably in the North-East midlands. The currency of the Speculum Vitae in Northern religious houses is shown also by the incorporation of parts of it in the Desert of Religion, a poem in which the "emblematic elements" are further developed, and meant to be seen as much as heard, which had limited circulation, it seems in nunneries and monasteries of the North Riding of Yorkshire.[21]

Furthermore, in identifying nearly 40 extant manuscripts of the Speculum Vitae, Doyle establishes that the poem circulated, not only in religious houses but among the nobility.[22] He also cites evidence from a colophon in MS. B. L. Ii. i. 36, dated from 1423, and overlooked by Allen, calling special attention to the alternate instructions--to read or hear--(underlining mine), as significant for an understanding of the intended audience and use of the Speculum Vitae:

> In minute letters at the head of an end-leaf: 'In die sanctorum crispini & crispiniani scribere incepi & die post festum annunciacionis beate marie finem habui Anno domini 1423'; and in apparently the same hand, larger, in the centre of another end-leaf: 'ӡe þat rede þis boke or here it redde. I pray ӡow praith for sir Roberte soule & alle cristen soulis. þat gaf þis boke to þis place. for wo so praith for anoðer. laburse for him selfe. and schal have grete mede.'[23]

Doyle's conclusion about the poem's circulation prior to 1384 was contested in 1976 by Venetia Nelson's hypothesis that the Cambridge approval was the impetus for the rapid dissemination of copies of the Speculum Vitae:

> This examination would have been virtually its imprimatur, its approval for publication. The copy read publicly at Cambridge would have been one of the very earliest manuscripts, perhaps the author's fair copy, with multiplication of copies following the official declaration of the poem's orthodoxy.[24]

Nelson's conclusion is conjecture, based on her study of the exemplars of the Vernon manuscript, whereas Doyle's study identifies owners, transmission, locality, and the probable audience of all the manuscripts of Nassington's poem. Doyle concludes that Nassington's theological contemporaries in Cambridge, in particular Chancellor John de Burgh, knew the scholarly value of the Speculum Vitae before 1384. Although it probably had significant circulation in clerical circles, Doyle argues that the Cambridge certification was a strong impetus for a wider distribution. The evidence I found about the biography of Nassington, establishing his death in 1359, coheres with Doyle's conclusion that the Speculum Vitae was widely circulated by 1384.

Literary Backgrounds and Imputed Sources

Three medieval traditions of instructional and devotional writing influenced the Speculum Vitae: the summa, the speculum including the catalogues of vices and virtues, and the Pater Noster schematizations. This mass of religious writing was the outcome of the reforms urged by the Fourth Lateran Council, and reflected the influence of scholasticism, with its systemization of religious knowledge by classification, definition, and division, and provided content and schemata for a wide range of derivative works--sermons, commentaries, glosses, prayers, and the great encyclopedic poems, such as William of Nassington's Speculum Vitae and the Cursor Mundi. These treatises of instruction and devotion were respositories of elementary dogma, moral theology, biblical history, and hagiography. Works from these three religious traditions have been named by scholars as Nassington's direct sources.

1. The Summa Tradition

The fourteenth century in England produced a large number of summae, compilations of canon law and moral theology which were used as instruction manuals by parish priests.[25] Bishop Robert Grosseteste's *Templum Domini* was one of several thirteenth-century forerunners of these compendia, and one of the most widely circulated, with 65 surviving manuscripts.[26] Combining a mastery of canon law with a genuine interest in pastoral theology, Grosseteste argued that theologians and priest canons were not removed from the pastoral needs of the people but were dedicated as clerical administrators. William of Pagula, vicar in the diocese of Salisbury in 1314, penitentiary for the deanery of Reading in 1332, and later penitentiary for the whole archdeaconry of Berkshire, wrote the *Oculus sacerdotis* (c. 1322); the *Summa summarum* (c. 1325-1327), a compendium of canon law and theology in five books and 257 chapters; the *Speculum prelatorum* (c. 1320-1326); and the *Speculum religiosorum* (c. 1320-1326).[27] W. A. Pantin calls him one of the few outstanding canonist writers of the later English Middle Ages, and the first author of a manual for English parish clergy to include diocesan legislation.[28] Apparently William of Pagula's *Oculus sacerdotis* appealed to the mystic Richard Rolle, for he incorporated some of its passages into his *Judica me deus*.[29] Moreover, William of Pagula's work was adapted by John de Burgh, Chancellor of the University of Cambridge, as his *Pupilla oculi* in 1385.[30]

The second half of the century brought additional, widely circulating *summa* intended for clergy and for educated lay audiences.[31] One of the most important was Archbishop Thoresby's

Instructions (1347), popularly known as the Lay Folks' Catechism.[32]
Thoresby was a civil servant, a chancery clerk, Keeper of the
Privy Seal and Chancellor, as well as Archbishop of York from
1352-1373. At his request John Gaytrick, a Benedictine monk of
St. Mary's in York, made an expanded English version of his
summa in verse, which included the fourteen articles of the creed,
ten commandments, seven sacraments, seven works of mercy, seven
virtues, and seven vices. Thoresby probably chose the verse
form for Gaytrick in order to popularize his instructional writing
and encourage memorization, and accordingly he provided incentive
for those who learned it by heart by offering an indulgence of
40 days remission of punishment in purgatory. At the end of the
century John Mirk, Prior of the Augustinian Priory of Lilleshall,
Salop, wrote the English verse Instructions for Parish Priests,
adapted, in part, from William of Pagula's Oculus sacerdotis.[33]
These thirteenth and fourteenth-century compilations set a
precedent for huge summa of church doctrine, such as the Speculum
Vitae.

Hope Emily Allen speculated that a lost Old French or
English summa might have been the source of the Speculum Vitae
and the Old French Somme le Roi.[34] Such a lost summa originally
had been suggested by R. E. Fowler as the source for the Somme
le Roi and Gower's Mirour de L'Omme. Allen further hypothesized
that Johannes Wallensis, one of the most conspicuous theologians
in both England and France during the fourteenth century, was a

likely author for such a summa.[35] My analysis of the Speculum Vitae in Chapters Three and Four illustrates that it is not taken from a single source, but the product of Nassington's scholarship and experience as a canon and mystic.

2. The Speculum Tradition

The speculum represents another prominent tradition in religious writing. Reviewing this tradition in medieval French manuscripts, A. Grabes lists more than 250 works which contain the word speculum, its French equivalent, miroir, or English mirror, in their titles.[36] In these works, speculum has two different meanings: the view of human nature made in the image and likeness of God, or as the view of God as the perfect divine model to be imitated by imperfect human nature. In the first sense, humanity is the mirror that manifests the invisible God, and the soul is the Imago Dei. In the second sense, imperfect humanity finds a mirror for perfection in God, especially in the example of Jesus Christ.[37] Thus speculum literature presents both an ideal of perfection and a model of instruction.

St. Augustine's Enarratio in psalmum 103 was a seminal text in establishing the medieval concept of speculum,[38] extending the model to include the mirror of Scripture. Hugh of St. Victor's twelfth-century commentary on the Rule of Augustine elaborates on the metaphor:

> Therefore, it is prescribed that you read this book until you know it by heart . . . . And it is rightly called a mirror; for we can see in it as a mirror in what state we

are, whether beautiful or deformed, just or unjust . . . .
For the Scriptures represent our interior picture to us,
showing us what is beautiful and what is deformed in the
soul, and how the beauty of justice ought to be observed
and how the ornament of the virtues ought to be prepared
as well as how the defilement of the vices ought to be
wiped away.[39]

Beginning in the thirteenth century, and as a result of the reform movement of the Fourth Lateran Council, the speculum as a mirror of vices and virtues informed many of the treatises on confession and penance. Examples of these include the very popular Le manuel des peches (c. 1260), an Anglo-Norman verse poem of over 12,000 lines by William of Waddington, a secular priest and official in the archiepiscopal court of York.[40] The Manuel was subsequently translated and versified in Handling Sin (1303), by Robert Mannyng of Brunne, a Gilbertine canon of Sempringham in Lincoln,[41] and reappeared in 1350 as Of Shrift and Penance.[42] A similar work, and one more closely related to the Speculum Vitae, was the Prick of Conscience (c. 1350), a long poem of over 4,812 couplets, which dealt with the wretchedness of man's state, of the world, and with the four last things: death, judgment, hell, and heaven.[43] Although the author of the Prick is unknown, at one time he was thought to be William of Nassington.

Several specula have been claimed as sources for Nassington's Speculum Vitae, based entirely on their similar treatments of the vices and virtues: the Somme des Vices et Vertues, or Somme le Roi (1235), by Frere Lorens d'Orleans, a thirteenth-century Dominican; a derivative text, the Miroir du Monde;[44] and the

Ayenbite of Inwyt (1340), by Dan Michel Northgate, which is a Kentish translation of the Somme.[45] That the Somme is the source of the Speculum Vitae was noted in the catalogue of the Vernon manuscript:

> The Mirror of Life; a poem generally attributed to William of Nassington, and founded on La Somme des Vices et des Vertues, of which there were two English prose translations in the fourteenth century, the one described under Art. 21 of this volume [Vernon catalogue]; the other known under the title Ayenbite of Inwyt, represented in a couplet at the end of the present poem:
>
> Prikke of Conscience hette this book,
> Whoso wol may rede and look.[46]

Allen's research led her to challenge these treatises on the vices and virtues as possible sources of the Speculum Vitae, as she gradually recognized its original structure and authorship.

In 1920 Hope Emily Allen suggested that the Speculum Vitae and the Ayenbite of Inwyt might be indebted to a common source:

> . . . allowing for the necessary differences between poetry and prose, the first three hundred lines of the Speculum Vitae and pp. 88-105 (Morris, ed. EETS, 23) of the Ayenbite of Inwyt may be said to be close enough to each other to make them appear to be translations from the same work; that is, practically everything in the Speculum Vitae can be found in the Ayenbite, though the reverse is not true.[47]

In 1917 Allen compared the Speculum Vitae, the Mirror of Life which is an English prose version of the Speculum Vitae, and the Somme le Roi. She illustrated how closely they were related with instances of parallel passages, but also drew attention to the original material in the Speculum Vitae:

> In the material in general the Middle-English Speculum and Mirror stand very near to the famous Somme of Frere

> Lorens, the source of the Ayenbite of Inwite. The
> Speculum has been said to be founded on the Somme,
> and again no comparison has been made; but enough
> has been done to show that the true relation is un-
> certain and complicated. Parts are identical, as
> the quotations at the end of this paper will prove,
> but again the Somme will give only the sketch of
> what is found in the Speculum. Most of the picturesque
> realism of the poem is derived from the Somme, but,
> on the other hand, the best of such material is new.
> In the prologue, as the quotations will show, the
> Speculum uses the Somme less than the tract on the
> Pater Noster, but the two latter for a few sentences
> coincide. What may be the general relation between
> these two sources is uncertain.[48]

According to Allen, the purported French source and the English works differ in their basic structure: the Pater Noster petitions appear toward the end of the Somme, whereas the Speculum Vitae and the Mirror of Life begin with a brief exposition of the Pater Noster, and then repeat the petitions as a structure for the body of the text. Thus, the entire Speculum Vitae is unified by the Pater Noster petitions. Of the other allied texts, Allen concludes that only the Somme le Roi and the Speculum Vitae are closely related.

My own comparisons of the Speculum Vitae with the Somme le Roi,[49] and its English translation, the Book of Vices and Virtues, refine Allen's findings about the unity of Nassington's poem. I found that the Somme is linear in its presentation of six indepen-dent units: the ten commandments, Apostles Creed, seven deadly sins, a treatise on death, the petitions of the Pater Noster, and the seven gifts of the Holy Spirit. While the Speculum Vitae is unified around the seven petitions of the Pater Noster, Allen failed to point out the centrality of the gifts of the Holy Spirit and the doctrine of grace in Nassington's work. The <u>Speculum Vitae</u> is not merely a more tightly organized version of the <u>Somme le Roi</u>, but an original treatment of the progressive spiritual life. The parallel passages quoted by Allen are commonplaces of the <u>speculum</u> of vices and virtues, and must be discounted as evidence of a source. In the <u>Somme le Roi</u> these lists of vices and virtues and their subdivisions have a didactic purpose, such as in the confessional manuals. In the <u>Speculum Vitae</u>, Nassington guides the reader from purgation of the vices, to illumination with the virtues, to perfection through the gifts of the Holy Spirit and the beatitudes.

3. The Pater Noster Tradition

The Pater Noster, with its seven petitions to the Father, became the vehicle for a wealth of artistic and theological interpretations in the Middle Ages.[50] This tradition had its origin in St. Augustine's <u>De Sermone Domini in monte</u>, where he linked the seven petitions, seven gifts of the Holy Spirit, and seven beatitudes, thereby establishing the following schema to illustrate the upward ascent of the soul toward perfection:

I	Hallowed be your name	Fear of the Lord	Blessed are the poor in spirit
II	Your kingdom come	Piety	Blessed are the meek
III	Your will be done	Knowledge	Blessed are they that mourn

IV	Give us our daily bread	Fortitude	Blessed are they that hunger
V	Forgive us our debts	Counsel	Blessed are the merciful
VI	Lead us not into temptation	Understanding	Blessed are the clean of heart
VII	Deliver us from evil	Wisdom	Blessed are the peacemakers

Augustine's fusion of petitions, gifts, and beatitudes into a model to restore the image of God in man's soul, drew together three patristic traditions:[51]

1. The petitions of the Our Father as found in the works of Cyprian, Tertullian, Origen, and Gregory of Nyssa.
2. The gifts of the Holy Spirit as found in the works of Ireneas of Lyon, Hilary, and Ambrose.
3. The beatitudes as found in the works of Gregory of Nyssa and Ambrose.

In the process of transmission to the Middle Ages, the Augustinian schema was modified by St. Gregory the Great (c. 540-604) in the <u>Moralia</u>, a commentary on the Book of Job that became a <u>summa</u> of dogma, moral asceticism, and mysticism. Gregory added the seven virtues--humility, friendship, equity, prowess, mercy, chastity, and soberness--and showed how they had power to eradicate the corresponding vices.[52] St. Gregory's emphasis on the subjugation of the vices by the virtues became the formula for later moral and ascetical writers. For example, Hugh of St. Victor (d. 1141) in his De quinque seu septem, further expanded the Augustinian schema to include the seven deadly sins--pride, envy, wrath, sloth, avarice, lechery, and gluttony--to form a pentad of sevens.[53] This pentad of interrelated sevens later informed Bishop Robert Grosseteste's popular Templum Domini.[54] Using the metaphor of the priest as doctor and the penitent as patient, Grosseteste prescribed the medicine of the petitions, beatitudes, and inclinations toward good, to restore health, that is, the seven virtues to the patient's soul. Grosseteste also employed the diagrammatic allegory of the tree of virtue and vice.

The continued popularity of the Pater Noster and its schema of sevens in the Middle Ages is established by Morton Bloomfield's monumental work, Incipits of Latin Works on the Virtues and Vices (1979).[55] After more than 20 years of research and with the help of three major collaborators, he compiled a list of more than 8,000 incipits of Latin works on the vices and virtues, and more than 2,000 additional incipits of Latin Pater Noster works. Such an abundance of similar material helps somewhat to preclude identifying any one text as the source of the Speculum Vitae.

Nonetheless, in 1969, Agnes David Gunn cited an anonymous Pater Noster tract, De Utilitate, along with these other possible sources for the Speculum Vitae: Somme le Roi, the Book of Vices and Virtues, Le Mireour du Monde, and the Form of Living.[56] Her hypothesis is that the Speculum Vitae is a conflation of the Somme le Roi, and De Utilitate, with its expansion of detail from the French source, its structure from the Latin text, and the long digression on the types of sin in lines 5595-5825 directly from the Form of Living. However, her conclusions rely on tangential textual similarities, such as the divisions of vices and virtues, which repeatedly appear in instructional and devotional writings. Furthermore, her evidence of parallel passages is far too slight to establish definitive source relationships with the Speculum Vitae.

Of similar importance, Gunn fails to establish a chronological basis for her assumption that the De Utilitate provided the source for the Speculum Vitae's structure. She worked from the text of the De Utilitate found in MS. B. L. Additional 15237, which the catalog dates in the fifteenth century.[57] The four other manuscripts containing texts of the De Utilitate are also much later than the 1384 terminus ad quem for the Speculum Vitae.[58] While these could represent fifteenth-century copies of an earlier text, in the absence of an earlier manuscript of the De Utilitate, Gunn's argument loses its force. The manuscript evidence indicates that, if the Latin text and the English poem are related, the relationship is either collateral, or the Speculum Vitae is the ultimate source. Hope Emily Allen offered such a conjecture about the relationship of the Speculum Vitae and the De Utilitate, which is as compelling now as in 1917.[59]

In addition, my examination of the De Utilitate and the Speculum Vitae indicates that the De Utilitate is considerably less inclusive than the Speculum.[60] It lacks discussions of the ten commandments, the twelve articles of faith, the cardinal and theological virtues, the corporal and spiritual works of mercy, and the active and contemplative life. Thus it does not begin to meet the didactic demands of the 1215 Fourth Lateran Council's call for reform as precisely as does the Speculum Vitae.

In the colophons in MSS. Royal 17 C. viii and Hatton 19, mentioned earlier, Nassington cites a Latin Pater Noster tract by John de Waldeby, Augustinian provincial, as his source for the Speculum Vitae. Following this Royal ascription, Warton gives Waldeby as Nassington's source.[61] Horstmann, too, concludes that Nassington's long poem, which he calls the Mirror of Life, is "a translation of John de Waldeby's Speculum Vitae."[62] In 1920, Hope Emily Allen began to consider Waldeby's connection with the Speculum Vitae:

> It should perhaps be noted, concerning John de Waldeby, that there seems some difficulty in connecting him with the Speculum Vitae on account of his late date. He is said (c. DNB) to have been the Provincial of the Augustinian Friars in England, and the brother of Robert Waldeby, archbishop of York, who died in 1398 (v. Lives of the Archbishops of York, ed. James Raine, Rolle Series, London, 1886, II, 428). He himself is said, in a manuscript note on the 'Trinity MS,' (Tanner, Biblio, Brit-Hib., p. 746, n.e), to have died in 1393. It may be remembered that Horstmann put the Tiberian manuscript of the Speculum Vitae at 1350. Some autobiographical details are said to be found in Waldeby's prologue addressed to the Abbot, St. Albans, which introduces his sermons in Caius Coll. Camb. MS. 334.[64]

It is important to my study that Allen, following Raine's Lives, placed Waldeby's death in 1393, an error which influenced her subsequent conclusions. In 1917 she compared the Speculum Vitae with Waldeby's Latin Commentary on the Pater Noster, concluded that it was not Nassington's source, and posited that Waldeby might have written a second commentary which might be the source of the Speculum Vitae.[64] She also hypothesized a scribal confusion between John de Waldeby and Joannes Wallensis who died in 1313 and, as a prolific writer, could have authored the source text. In 1921 Warner and Gilson's Catalogue of Royal Manuscripts supported Allen's conclusion about Waldeby, examined other Waldeby writings, and noted that they also had little in common with the Speculum Vitae.[65]

Aubrey Gwynn's chapter on John Waldeby in the English Austin Friars provides a full account of his life and his importance as a religious leader:

> On 26 March 1349 Simon Waldeby is one of the three Austin friars whom Archbishop William La Zouche admitted as confessors in the archdiocese (Reg. Zouche, fol. 278b). Nothing further seems to be known of this friar, but he was probably an elder brother of John Waldeby, who was appointed as penitentiary for the city of York by La Zouche's successor, Archbishop Thoresby, on 12 October 1354. (Reg. Thoresby, fol. 29b). In this document Waldeby is described as sacre theologie professor; he must have been admitted to the magisterium of Oxford or Cambridge before that date . . . . Turning to Bale's Scriptores Illustres Maioris Brytanniae we find John Waldeby described as a distinguished graduate of Oxford who won special honour at some academic function (solemnitate quadam) which is not further defined.[66]

Based on John Waldeby's appointment as penitentiary of York in 1354, Gwynn conjectured that his tenure of office as Augustinian provincial was before 1357, although he continued to flourish as a writer after that time. Since no work of Waldeby's has survived which is not named in the 1372 catalogue of the York library, Gwynn concluded that he died soon after that. No record of Waldeby exists later than 1372, with the exception of the erroneous death date in 1392, where his name was substituted by the scribe of <u>Fascicule Zizaniorum</u> for the younger Robert Waldeby. Gwynn's chapter reveals the importance of considering Waldeby and Nassington as contemporary ecclesiastical servants. Waldeby was appointed as penitentiary of York, and served as Augustinian provincial during Nassington's service as Archbishop William Zouche's chancellor, placing Waldeby under Nassington as visitor and presumably occasioned their meetings.

In addition to his important religious positions, Waldeby was a highly esteemed author of letters, sermon collections, and devotional treatises, all written in Latin. In 1365, Waldeby compiled a collection of his sermons for the Sundays of the ecclesiastical year, entitled <u>Novum opus dominicale</u>. Gwynn also attributes to him a sermon collection for the principal liturgical feasts. Besides these two compilations, the library of York held a <u>Repertorium Waldeby</u>, which was apparently a manual for use of preachers. Three series of homilies are extant today: a series of seven on the Pater Noster, which are homilies on the seven deadly sins; five on the Ave Maria; and a more elaborate set of twelve on the articles of the Apostles Creed. All were popular in England in the fourteenth and fifteenth century.

John Waldeby was closely linked with Abbot Thomas de la Mare, who ruled the Benedictine monastary of St. Alban's from 1349 to 1396 and who was, according to Gwynn, the most powerful Benedictine of the fourteenth century and one of the most distinguished prelates of his generation:

> [He was] the son of Sir John de la Mare, and was connected with several noble families: including the La Zouche family, which had given York its archbishop in the preceding generation, and the Grandisson family, which gave Exeter a famous bishop at this time.[67]

In 1354 at Thomas' request, Waldeby arranged a collection of his sermons, and dedicated it, as well as his tract on the Creed, to the Abbot. Given the duties of these three prominent churchmen--Nassington the chancellor of York, Waldeby the Augustinian provincial, and Thomas the Abbot of St. Alban's--it would appear likely that they knew each other and each other's writings. The same fraternal spirit in which Waldeby dedicated his work to Thomas may have led Nassington to dedicate his writing to Waldeby through the colophon announcing Waldeby's Pater Noster tract as the Latin source of the Speculum Vitae. Such a conclusion extends the direction of Allen's thought, supported by the crucial biographical data which deterred her scholarship on Nassington.

Finally, the relationship must be clarified between the Speculum Vitae and English prose Mirror of Life, contained in MSS. Harley 45, Bodleian E. 35, and Rawlinson A. 335.[68] A fourth copy, entitled A Myrour to Lewde Man and Women was found in a manuscript purchased by the library of the University of Pennslyvania in 1950.[69] In 1952

Edna Stover made a line-by-line comparison of the Speculum Vitae and the Myrour and concluded "beyond all doubt" that the poetic Speculum was the source of the prose Myrour:

> In that the Myrour is a reduction of a poem to prose, it follows an unusual technique in Middle English literature, for whereas in the thirteenth century it was the fashion for French writers to write "desrime," and in the fifteenth century in England there is a growing tendency to write original works in prose rather than in verse, very few instances can be found in Middle English literature of verse so directly converted into prose.[70]

In 1978 Venetia Nelson, after studying the text of the Speculum Vitae in MS. Cotton Tiberius E. VII, posited the opposite view, that the prose Mirror of Life was the source of the verse Speculum.[71] Her view was based on preparation of an edition of a 4,000-line section of the Speculum Vitae in one manuscript, where her primary interest is in the interference of the scribe in the author's text. At no time does she provide firm evidence to support her assumption regarding the precedence of the Mirror over the Speculum.

A. I. Doyle concurred with Stover's conclusion, and explained that the Speculum Vitae was so well-known and appreciated in the households and convents of England in the fourteenth century that there was little demand for the Myrour, "its weaker prose rival."[72] My research shows how Nassington's ecclesiastical knowledge and experience is integral to the content, design, and exempla of the Speculum Vitae, all characteristics marking its originality as a text and confirming the position of Stover and Doyle.

What then can be said for the origin of the Speculum Vitae? The source studies referred to in this chapter show not only that much of its content can be traced to commonplaces in medieval writings on the vices and virtues but also that it differs from any imputed source in significant aspects. The inability to identify any one single source suggests that it is a compilation, unified into a work more integrated than its predecessors or analogues, by incorporating the theology of the gifts of the Holy Spirit as the root of perfection. Allen, at the culmination of her source studies, viewed the poem primarily as an English creation, compiled by a poet of wide intellectual range and competence in canon law and theology and with insight into human nature. She concluded:

> However far the Speculum Vitae may appear to us to-day from the type of work to which an academic sanction would be granted, there can be no doubt that it represented some of the best theology of its time, worked over, as it seems, by a compiler of some talent.[73]

> By its attachment to the Pater Noster of the whole theology and ethics of the Church, as they concern laymen, it is a triumph of the mediaeval art of hanging a universal theology to the exposition of texts, and it would seem that its carefully articulated schematism solved the general problem of what might be called the architechtonics of the Summa for laymen,-- which was a form of literature for which the ecclesiastical statutes kept alive the demand, and to some extent fixed the elements.[74]

My research on the biography of William of Nassington confirms that he had such a background, and even more, that he was a distinguished prelate with first-hand knowledge of church and diocesan affairs.

The Speculum Vitae enjoyed a significance in the English medieval church that has not been acknowledged sufficiently by contemporary scholarship. It should be viewed with Edmund Rich's Mirror of Holy

Church, the most popular and widely circulated religious writing of the thirteenth century.[75] Like the Mirror, the Speculum Vitae was a guide to Christian salvation and perfection, teaching that self-knowledge comes from reflection on the goodness of God, the example of Christ, knowledge of the Scriptures, and prayer and contemplation. More popular than their solely didactic counterparts, for two centuries these catechetical and mystical treatises sought to fulfill the spiritual needs of a deeply religious people.

NOTES

[1] Thomas Warton, History of English Poetry, III, ed., Sir F. Madden, (London, 1840), (rpt. Hildesheim, Georg Olms, 1968), p. 116.

[2] Allen, "The Authorship of the Prick of Conscience," Studies in English and Comparative Literature (Boston: Ginn, 1910), p. 167, n. 1.

[3] George F. Warner and Julius P. Gilson, Catalogue of Western Manuscripts on the Old Royal and King's Collections, II (1921), p. 240.

[4] Joseph Ritson, ed., Bibliographia Poetica, A Catalog of English Poets of the 12th, 13th, 14th, 15th, and 16th Centuries, London: Roward, 1802, p. 91-92. Ritson explains the common practice of the age for the copyist of a poem to insert his name as author. He cites several examples from John Lydgate, as the "Life of the Virgin Mary," where it concludes, "Here endeth the life of oure lady. Quod Johannes Forster," and a MS. of Rolle's poems in T.C.D. in which the transcriber claims the poem has on this account become the property of John Flemyng.

[5] Hope Emily Allen, Writings Ascribed to Richard Rolle and Materials for his Biography, (New York: Heath, 1917), p. 371.

[6] "Studien zu Richard Rolle de Hampole," Englische Studien 7 (1884), p. 415-72.

[7] "The Authorship of the Prick of Conscience," p. 168.

[8] "The Speculum Vitae; Addendum," PMLA 32 (1917), p. 135-36.

[9] "The Speculum Vitae," p. 134, n.3.

[10] Allen, p. 134, n.3. A. I. Doyle's unpublished research shows that many of these incomplete versions can be attributed to the nature of the poem for, it was useful in individual sections, so that it may have been copied in part, depending upon its use.

[11] Allen, p. 136.

[12] Allen, p. 372.

[13] A. I. Doyle, "A Survey of the Origins and Circulation of the Theological Writings in English in the 14th, 15th, and early 16th Centuries," Diss. Cambridge Univ. 1953, p. 81. The Bande of Lovyng in MS. Thornton is the same poem as the Tractatus de Trinitate et Unitate in MS. Cotton Tiberius E. VII; both have ascriptions to Nassington which identify him as advocate from York.

[14] Helsinki: Societé Néophilologique, 1972, 2n, 13.

[15] C. Horstmann, ed., Yorkshire Writers, Richard Rolle of Hampole, II (London: Swan Sonnenschein, 1896), p. 274.

[16] H. L. D. Ward, vol. II (London: Longmans, 1892), p. 746, Ullmann, Englische Studien, 7 (1884), p. 416, quoted in Francis A. Foster, ed., The Northern Passion: French Text, Variants and Fragments, etc. EETS 147 (1916), p. 5; John E. Wells, A Manual of the Writings in Middle English 1050-1400 (New Haven: Yale University Press, 1916); Carleton Brown and Rossell Hope Robbins, Index of Middle English Verse, II, (Oxford: Clarendon Press, 1943), p. 40; Nelson, "Cot. Tiberius E. VII: A Manuscript of the Speculum Vitae," English Studies, 59 (1978), p. 97; Herbert, Catalogue of Romances, III, p. 331, cited in Foster, p. 18, also gives 1400 as the date for Cottom Tiberius.

[17] Trans. in W. A. Pantin, The English Church in the Fourteenth Century (Cambridge: University Press, 1955), p. 229. The Latin text appears in Allen, PMLA, 32 (1917), p. 148.

[18] Allen, p. 148, trans. Wilkins, Concilia Magnae Britanniae, III (London, 1730), pp. 314-19, also pp. 338, 365, 378.

[19] Knyghton under the date 1382, says that half the population was Wycliffite (Chronicon, Rolls Series, London, 1895, II), p. 85, in Allen, "The Speculum Vitae," p. 149, n.45.

[20] Doyle, p. 85.

[21] Doyle, p. 85. MS. Royal is dated 1418, which is confirmed in other listings; Wells, p. 463, concludes that since MS. Royal is dated 1418, Nassington probably flourished about 1375; Pollard, DNB, XIV (1921), p. 120, gives 1418; Owst, noted in Ch. 1, dates Nassington and the Speculum Vitae from the 1384 date of the Cambridge certification and does not advert to MS. Royal.

[22] Brown and Robbins, Index of Middle English Verse (Oxford: Clarendon Press, 1943), p. 245, list 35 manuscripts. Doyle, p. 83, updates their list and indicates the location of some of the Speculum Vitae manuscripts: "the Southeby-Maggs copy now Bodl. Lyell MS., 28; the Quaritch one now Liverpool Univ.; Lord Middleton's (Wollaston Hall) now in Nottingham Univ. Lib. TDC is possibly Saville 32 (N.25). There was a copy in the Earl of Kingston's MSS., later burned, at Thoresby House (Notts.), CC 18 (no. 877 in Phillipps' Cat.). Neither of the last two, nor the Petre MS. mentioned below in IMEV," nor Sr. Agnes David Gunn, "Accidia and Prowess in the Vernon Version of Nassyngton's Speculum Vitae: An Edition of the Text and Study of the Ideas," Diss., University of Pennsylvania, 1969, P. 1, n.2, mentions a manuscript owned by Mr. Robert Taylor, Princeton, sold at Southeby March 10, 1952. Smeltz amends Brown and Robbins' list by identifying 28 and 29 as British Museum manuscripts. He notes a fragment from the Malborough Vicarage, and dates the Southby sale as June 18, 1940, Item 522. In addition to these poetic versions, four prose Speculum have been identified. Hope Emily Allen, "The Speculum Vitae; An Addendum," PMLA, 32, (1917), p. 156, names the Miroir, from Harl. MS. 45, and Bodl. E. Mus. 35ff pp. 221-242, and Rawl. MS. A. P. 346, all fifteenth-century prose versions. Edna M. Stover, "Myrour to Lewde Men and Wymmen, A Note on a Recently Acquired Manuscript," University of Pennsylvania Library Chronicle, 16, (1950), pp. 81-86, identifies a fourth prose manuscript, acquired from a London bookseller in 1949, now housed in the Rare Book Collection in the University of Pennsylvania Library, and made available by Stover in a dissertation in 1952, "An Edition of the Middle English Treatise, A Myrour to Lewde Man and Wymmen." Venetia Nelson's edition of Myrour to Lewde Men and Wymenn has been published by Carl Winter Verlag, Heidelberg, 1982.

[23] Doyle, p. 85, n.17

[24] "The Vernon and Simeon Copies of the Speculum Vitae," English Studies, 57 (1976), p. 390-391.

[25] For a complete treatment of these instructional manuals see Pantin, Chapter IX, "Manuals of Instruction for Parish Priests," pp. 189-219, G. H. Russell, "Vernacular Instruction of the Laity in the Later Middle Ages in England; Some Texts and Notes," Journal of Religious History, 2 (1962), p. 98-119; H. G. Pfander, "Some Medieval Manuals of Religious Instruction in England and Observations on Chaucer's Parson's Tale," JEGP, 35 (1936), p. 243-58; H. G. Pfander, "The Mediaeval Friars and Some Alphabetical Reference Books for Sermons," Medium Aevum, 3 (1934), p. 19-29; G. R. Owst, Part Three "The Sermons," Preaching in Medieval England (Cambridge: University Press, 1926), pp. 222-354; Kate O. Petersen, Sources of the Parson's Tale, Radcliffe College Monographs, 12 (Boston, Ginn, 1901, rpt, New York: AMS, 1973); R. E. Fowler, Une Source française des poèmes de Gower (Macon, 1905); also consult P. S. Jolliffe, A Check List of Middle English Prose Writings of Spiritual Guidance (Toronto: Pontifical Institute of Mediaeval Studies, 1974).

[26] See S. Harrison Thomson, The Writings of Robert Grosseteste (Cambridge, 1940), pp. 138-40, and Pantin, p. 193. Pantin, p. 219, lists the following summae or manuals of pastoral theology which were produced in England in the thirteenth century and were the forerunners of the manuals that he discusses: 1) the Summa 'Res grandis' of Robert Flamborough, written at the request of Richard Poore, c. 1208-10; it is a penitential; 2) the Summa 'Cum miseraciones Domini' of Thomas of Chabham, sub-deacon of Salisbury, written c. 1215-22; pastoral as well as penitential; 3) the Summa 'Qui bene presunt' by Richard Wethershed, chancellor of Cambridge, written c. 1220-29; 4) the Summa 'Signaculum apostolatus mei, a manual for prelates, written perhaps c. 1245-50; 5) the Summa 'Templum Domini' of Robert Grosseteste, written c. 1238-45; 6) the Summa 'Speculum Iuniorum' written c. 1250-60; 7) the Summa 'Ad instructionem iuniorum' of Simon of Hinton, O. P., written c. 1250-60; 8) the Summa 'Animarum regimen,' a short treatise on confessional practice, written c. 1250-70. Pantin credits Fr. Leonard Boyle, O. P., with this list.

[27] Pantin, p. 195.

[28] Pantin, p. 196.

[29] Allen, Writings Ascribed to Richard Rolle, p. 101.

[30] Pantin, p. 213.

[31] Pantin, pp. 202-18, includes discussions of the Cilium Oculi, Speculum Curatorum (1340), ascribed to Ranulph Higden, monk of Chester; Regimen Animarum (1343); Memoriale Presbiterorum (1344), by a doctor of canon law at Avignon; Mirk's Manuale Sacerdotis and Festial.

[32] T. F. Simmons and H. E. Nolleth, eds, (EETS, 118) including the Latin and English version together with the Lollard version.

[33] Pantin, p. 212.

[34] Allen, p. 146.

[35] Allen, p. 146, n.32.

[36] Herbert Grabes, "Speculum, Mirror und Looking-Glass," Kontinuität und Originalität der Spiegelmetapher in den Buchtiteln des Mittelalters und der englischen Literatur des 13. bis 17 Jahrhunderts, (Tübingen, 1973), cité, Grabes offre cependant une bonne vue d'ensemble (en appendice, répertoire des Miroirs en latin en diverses langues, pp. 246-351), in "Miroir," Dictionnaire de spiritualité ascétique et mystique doctrine et histoire, eds. Marcel Viller et al., unpublished volumne, p. 1292.

[37] See the article "Miroir" by Margot Schmidt in the forthcoming volume of Dictionnaire de spiritualité, p. 1291-1302.

[38] See Ritamary Bradley, "Backgrounds of the Title Speculum in Mediaeval Literature," Speculum, 29 (1954), pp. 100-15.

[39] "Expositio in Regulam Beati Augustini," PL, CLXXVI, 923D-924A), trans. in Bradley, p. 111.

[40] E. J. Arnould, ed., Le manuel des peches (Paris, 1940).

[41] J. Furnivall, ed., EETS, 119 (1901), 123 (1903).

[42] See Arnould, pp. 319-34, in Pantin, p. 225.

[43] R. Morris, ed., Philological Society (Berlin, 1863).

[44] Felix Chavannes, ed., Le Miroir de Monde (Lasuanne, 1845).

[45] Phyllis Gradon, ed., Dan Michael's Ayenbite of Inwyt or Remorse of Conscience, Richard Morris' transcription now newly collated with the uniques Manuscript British Museum MS. Arundel 57 (EETS, 23, 1886, reissued 1965). Nelson W. Francis orders the texts related to the Somme le Roi, based upon the earlier scholarship of Meyer and Tinberger (in Romania between 1900-1910, in The Book of Vices and Virtues; a Fourteenth Century English Translation of the Somme le Roi of Lorens D' Orléans, (EETS, 217, 1942), ix-lxxxi. See also Edith Brayer, "Contendu, Structure et combinaisons du Miroir du Monde et de la Somme le Roi," Romania, 79 (1958), 1-38.

[46] Allen, "Authorship of the Prick of Conscience," pp. 168-69.

[47] Allen, p. 169, n. 1.

[48] Allen, "The Speculum Vitae," pp. 143-44.

[49] A. B. Tysor, ed., "Somme des Vices et Vertues, "Part I," University of North Carolina, 1949; E. J. Allen, ed., "Somme des Vices et Vertues, Part II," University of North Carolina, 1951.

[50] See Maurice Hussey, "The Petitions of the Paternoster in Medieval English Literature," Medium Aevum, 27 (1958), 8-16, for a chronological summary of the Pater Noster literature and didactic art forms in manuscript illuminations. The schema in my text is adapted from Hussey, p. 8, using Augustine's De sermone Domini in monte, in PL, 34, 1276-308.

[51] This summary of the development of the patristic tradition is based on John Smeltz, "Speculum Vitae: An Edition of British Museum Manuscript Royal 17 C. viii," Diss. Duquesne University, 1977, pp. 1-35. These three points are adapted from page 30. He suggests that the two essential elements which are found in Augustine's De sermone, the beatitudes as a program of Christian perfection and the symbolic significance of the numbers seven and eight, are found in the works of Gregory of Nyssa, and could very well have been transmitted to St. Augustine by St. Ambrose.

[52] Smeltz contends that Augustine's concept of the Our Father as a means for ascending to God and the petitions as a means of representing different levels of the spiritual life appears to be based in the five homilies of Gregory delivered in Lent in 385 A.D.

[53] Pantin, p. 227, cites Hugh of Victor (in PL, CLXXV, 405), who provides an even more complex version of the seven by dividing the beatitudes into two sections, those who are blessed and the blessing they receive. See the description of his Ad instructionem iuniorum (c 1260), in Recherches de Théologie ancienne et médiévale, 9, (1937), p. 6. Smeltz traces Dante's use of the schema of the seven sins in the journey in the Purgatorio, where the seven P's are erased beginning with the Lord's prayer, and where he collates the vices, virtues, and beatitudes, p. 18. Also see Wenzel, "Dante's Rationale for the Seven Deadly Sins," Modern Language Review, 60 (1964), pp. 529-33.

[54] Grosseteste, quoted from Bodleian 631, fol. 186v-87, in Pantin, p. 228. Pantin divides his discussion of religious and moral treatises in the vernacular into five groups, placing Nassington's Speculum Vitae with those which attempt to equate the various groups of sevens.

[55] Morton W. Bloomfield, ed., et al., (Cambridge, Mass.: The Mediaeval Academy of America, 1979).

[56] Agnes David Gunn, "Accidia and Prowess in the Vernon Version of Nassyngton's Speculum Vitae," Diss. University of Pennsylvania, 1969, p. 13.

[57] British Museum, Department of Manuscripts, Catalogue of the Additions to the Manuscripts of the British Museum (London, 1841-1845), pp. 117-18.

[58] The De Utilitate appears in four other manuscripts: B. L. Rawlinson C. 72, Burney 356, Harleian 1022 and 1648, given in Bloomfield.

[59] Allen, "The Speculum Vitae," p. 147.

[60] De Utilitate Orationis Dominicae, Bodleian Manuscript, Rawlinson, C. 72, in Gunn, pp. 240-281.

[61] Warton, p. 116.

[62] Horstman, II, p. 274.

[63] Allen, p. 169, n. 1.

[64] Allen, "The *Speculum Vitae*," pp. 36-37. Bloomfield identifies one other possible Pater Noster treatise by Waldeby and the "Septies in die laudem dixi tibi, Ps. 118, 164," no. 9123, p. 672. The Pater Noster tract, consisting of three principal parts, a prohemium, tract, and a conclusion, is identified in ten manuscripts, averaging twenty-five to fifty folio pages, and is listed by Bloomfield with its alternate incipits, no. 8092, p. 575.

[65] Warner and Gilson, II, p. 240.

[66] Gwynn, Oxford, 1940, p. 114.

[67] Gwynn, p. 119.

[68] Noted in Allen, "The *Speculum Vitae*," p. 155, and Pantin, p. 228.

[69] "A Myrour to Lewde Men and Wymmen," "A Note on a Recently Acquired Manuscript," *PULC*, 6 (1950).

[70] "A Myrour to Lewde Men and Wymmen," Diss. Pennsylvania University, 1951, p. 3.

[71] "Cot. Tiberius E. VII: A Manuscript of the *Speculum Vitae*," pp. 112-13.

[72] Doyle, p. 92.

[73] Allen, "The Speculum Vitae," p. 153.

[74] Allen, p. 155.

[75] Helen P. Forshaw, ed., *Edmund of Abingdon; Speculum Religiosorum and Speculum Ecclesie* (London: Oxford University Press, 1973).

CHAPTER III

THE SPECULUM VITAE AS A DIDACTIC COMPENDIUM

William of Nassington's 16,396-line Speculum Vitae is both a compendium of ecclesiastical doctrine prescribed by the reform movement and a guide to the spiritual life through purgation, illumination, and mystical union. The didactic elements described in this chapter constitute the schematic framework, which includes the Seven Petitions, Gifts of the Holy Spirit, Vices, Virtues, and Beatitudes, and embodies other dogma, such as the Ten Commandments and the Seven Sacraments, prescribed by the English councils. Chapter Four demonstrates how Nassington draws upon this didactic framework, superimposing an elaborate treatise on perfection, which explains the spiritual exercises and type of progressive prayer for the beginner, intermediate, and mystic. The Speculum Vitae reveals Nassington's comprehensive scholarship. Because the Speculum Vitae synthesizes the instructional, schematic, and devotional writings of centuries in the most complete orthodox manual compiled, it is important as a speculum of fourteenth-century religious England.

As a didactic compendium, the Speculum Vitae incorporates features of its fourteenth-century predecessors: the Summa, Speculum of Vices and Virtues, and the schema of Pater Noster

Petitions. A description of the structure and content of the Speculum Vitae reveals its relationship to the schematized Somme le Roi and its derivative texts. These treatises, termed by Pantin as "curious experiments in theological mathematics," represent the popular tradition of Vices and Virtues.[1] However, Nassington's Speculum Vitae moves beyond the heptamerology and incorporates a theology of salvation and perfection through sanctifying grace.

The central theological construct of the Speculum Vitae is the doctrine of sanctifying grace derived from the works of Augustine on the operations of the Holy Spirit and the doctrine of Thomas Aquinas on the promptings of the Spirit. The Speculum Vitae incorporates Augustine's doctrine that the beatitudes are moral counsels for all Christians, forming a perfect rule of life impelled by the new law of love, and Thomas' doctrine of grace, demonstrating how the Gifts of the Holy Spirit are the essential action of the spiritual life. No one before Thomas had characterized the Gifts as movements of the Spirit which empower the human mind through faith to lead a life transcending natural ability.[2] Through grace the Christian participates in the life of God and begins to work toward his ultimate goal, union with God. Through grace he realizes his highest purpose--to restore the Imago Dei his soul, clouded by sin.

Nassington insists that the Gifts of the Spirit provide the grace which teaches, guides, and strengthens human nature to participate in God's life as his adopted sons. The <u>Speculum Vitae</u> demonstrates that the height of the spiritual perfection, expressed as that "Whilk festyns þe hert ay fast/In Gode þe fadir ay to last (2372-73)" is within the reach of all persons, learned and lewd, including those who read Latin and those who do not. Nassington links the Petitions of the Pater Noster to the Gifts of the Spirit, following Thomas' teaching that these Gifts bestow the grace promised by Christ to all his disciples. Therefore, all who seek perfection, including the unlettered, are identified as the audience for the <u>Speculum Vitae</u>:

>   Tharfor, I holde it mast sekyr þan
>   To shew the langage that ilk man,
>   And alle, for lewede mens sake anely,
>   That cane no maner of clergy,
>   To kene þame it ware mast nede,
>   For clerkys cane both se & rede
>   In sere boks of haly wyrte
>   How þai salle lyfe, if that luke it;
>   Þarfor, wille I me hally halde
>   To that langage that ynglych is calde (82-92).

Such a broad audience is also suggested by the variety of topical exempla in the <u>Speculum Vitae</u>, which concerns a wide spectrum of representatives ranging from tavern dweller to nobleman.

Nassington's text gives clues to his audience and to the intended use of the <u>Speculum Vitae</u>. From a variety of passages scattered throughout the poem, other inferences can be made. Early in the work, he addresses his audience, "you, that me herys also swa (12)," and "Goode men and women (20)." A time is suggested, "And while I spake kepe you fro slepp (33)," and place:

> For we shuld alle, with hert stedfast,
> Do Gode alle maner of reueraunce,
> And namely her in his presence,
> In kyrk, and other stedys with out
> Þar his body is born a bout (472-477).

He invites them not only as listeners, but also as readers:

> As men may fynde in þis buke
> Aftyr ward, who so wille luke (448-449).

This passage and his allusions to the romances suggest an informal audience, one conversant with the legendary heroes: Sir Isumbras, Octovan, the Anglo-Norman Bevis of Hamptoun, and the popular Guy of Warwick, the knight who became a pilgrim and a hermit in retribution for his worldly life (37-47). The English versions of these romances are found in manuscripts from the first half and middle of the fourteenth century, which corroborates the dates for Nassington established in Chapter One.[3]

A. I. Doyle's scholarship, describes the manuscripts of the Speculum Vitae, traces the common medieval practice of separating portions of poems to be used not only as sermons and homilies, but also for private readings in convents and households of devout noble women.[4] For example, the Vernon and Simeon manuscripts were intended for both public and private use, since both contain verse sermons for liturgical and communal occasions as well as devotional pieces.[5] When the overwhelming oral tradition of the thirteenth and fourteenth centuries gave way to private reading, the Speculum Vitae served the growing masses of literate laity. Doyle's research shows that many of the manuscripts including copies of the Speculum Vitae were possessed by religious houses or the nobility, and probably placed in a chapel, hall, or refectory. Many devout women, including those under religious vows, were unable to read Latin and were, therefore, an eager audience for a vernacular guide to the spiritual life. Thus the popularity of the Speculum Vitae evinces the religious climate of late medieval England.

The Structure and Organization of the Speculum Vitae

The Pater Noster with its seven Petitions provides the framework for the schematization of the major content of the Speculum Vitae. There are three Expositions of the Pater Noster Petitions in the entire poem, two in the Introduction and a third lengthy Exposition that constitutes the body of the work. In each Exposition, Nassington divides the Petitions into two categories, separating the first three, which name spiritual concerns, from the last four, which name temporal concerns. But in the Third Exposition, the order of the Petitions is inverted, with the discussion of the four Petitions asking for temporal goods placed before the discussion of the three Petitions asking for spiritual goods. In the body of the Speculum Vitae, Nassington gives only 2,605 lines to the four temporal petitions, while he devotes 10,154 lines to the three spiritual petitions. Nassington's emphasis on the advanced stages of perfection is illustrated by the following outline of the entire plan of the Speculum Vitae, indicating the number of lines given to each section:

> First Exposition   2196 lines
> Second Exposition   1001 lines
> Third Exposition   12,889 lines

The First Exposition includes most of the doctrine required by the reform, the Second Exposition explains the doctrine of sanctifying grace, and the Third Exposition stresses union with God as the eternal goal of earthly existence.

The Introduction to the <u>Speculum Vitae</u> begins with a peroration and includes two preliminary Expositions of the Pater Noster Petitions. The peroration (1-205) incorporates the following conventional material:

> Invocation
> Statement of the author's unworthiness
> Moral purpose of the work
> Defense of the vernacular language
> Significance of the mirror image
> Preview of content and structure

In the Invocation, Nassington calls upon God the Father as First Person of the Trinity for grace to accomplish his over-all purpose -- to move his audience to divine love. The Invocation is followed by his statement of unworthiness, the modesty <u>topos</u> which usually introduces such a work. He requests the prayers of the audience, as he in turn prays for those who hear his counsel. Next, Nassington distinguishes his work from the episodic romances read as court entertainments. In contrast to such works, the <u>Speculum Vitae</u> has a moral purpose:

> How ȝe salle reule here ȝour lyue,
> (And goune) wele ȝour wytts fyue,
> How ȝe shalle folow Godds wille,
> And lere to knawe both good & ille,
> And what ȝe shall chese, and what forasyke
> And what way ȝe shalle to hewyn take (56-71).

In accordance with the widespread practice in the fourteenth century of using the vernacular for religious writings, Nassington's English guide to perfection is addressed to a large audience (62-92). He then tells them about the importance of the image of the speculum:

> Good men undirstandys me now
> The right way I salle kene ȝow
> That ȝe may hold while ȝe lyfe,
> And swylk a lesson I salle ȝou gyf
> That myroure of lyf to ȝou may be
> In whilk ȝe may alle ȝour lyfe se (92-97).

Following this brief peroration, Nassington introduces his three Expositions of the Pater Noster Petitions. Each is preceded by a plea for the right understanding of the Pater Noster. In the First Exposition, Nassington asks that the Pater Noster be prayed with the faculty of Understanding; in the Second Exposition, that it be prayed with the faculty of Reason; and in the Third Exposition, that it be prayed with the faculty of the Will. In each of these three Expositions, Nassington gives a summary of the entire schema of the <u>Speculum Vitae</u>, and then names and comments on each Pater Noster Petition by relating it to other church doctrine. The importance of the Trinity in the <u>Speculum Vitae</u>, even as the subject of the incipit, suggests a symbolic design in this trinity of threes:

<u>First Exposition</u> (98-2294)
Summary of schema of Sevens
Praying the Pater Noster with Understanding
Exposition of the Seven Petitions

Second Exposition (2295-3306)
Praying the Pater Noster with Reason
Summary of schema of Sevens
Exposition of the Seven Petitions

Third Exposition (3307-16,396)
Praying the Pater Noster with the Will
Summary of the schema of Sevens
Exposition of the Seven Petitions

First Exposition of the Pater Noster Petitions (98-2294)

Nassington begins the First Exposition of the Pater Noster Petitions with an announcement of the entire plan of the <u>Speculum Vitae</u>, telling how the Seven Petitions ask for the Seven Gifts of the Holy Spirit, which replace the Seven Vices with the Seven Virtues and bring the merits and rewards of the Seven Beatitudes:

> And specialy of the sevene askyngs
> That on the <u>pater noster</u> hyngs,
> And of sevene gyfts of þe Haly Gast
> That sevene askynges may to us hast,
> And of sevene synnes that mast may smert
> That þe sevene gyfts putts out of hert,
> And specialy of vertous sevene,
>
> That may be sett in þer stede evene,
> And of the seven blyssed hedys
> To whilk the seven vertuous us leyds,
> And to the seven medys alle
> That to be blyssed hedys shuld falle (102-113).

After explaining how the Pater Noster provides the structure for the <u>Speculum Vitae</u>, Nassington describes its profit, fruit, and dignity (116-209), a commonplace in tracts on the Lord's Prayer, with a discourse similar to the ones in the <u>Somme le Roi</u> and its related texts. Understanding, a Gift of Spirit and faculty of the soul, Nassington argues, is essential for one who would pray the Pater

Noster with devotion. He deplores those who have knowledge of the "naked letter" of the Pater Noster, but who do not feel its spirit with devotion (147-191). The spiritual life begins with the effort of the understanding in prayer:

> Undirstand, and in hert knytt;
> It is alswa lyght to say,
> For men shuld thrught it often pray;
> Suttelle to undirstand is it,
> For men shulde mare sett þer wytt
> On the sentence of it namely
> Trugh grett besynes and study (185-191)

In this First Exposition, Nassington establishes the pattern of dividing the Petitions of the Pater Noster into two groups, the spiritual and the temporal. The first three Petitions ask for spiritual goods: the grace of final perseverance expressed as "festenyng of our herts to stand in gode (238-39)," the coming of the kingdom, and the fulfillment of God's will. The next four petitions ask for temporal goods: daily bread, forgiveness of the past, deliverance from present harm, and the avoidance of future evil. Thus, the three spiritual Petitions focus on eternity, whereas the four temporal Petitions measure time as past, present and future.

Nassington's paraphrase of the Pater Noster and the brief comment on each Petition in the First Exposition is followed by a longer commentary on the words that introduce the petitions, Pater Noster Qui Es In Celis, which Nassington calls the Prologue. The didactic topics that Nassington weaves into this discussion refer to subjects previously introduced in the section on the understanding and utility of the Pater Noster, and look forward to topics that will be presented more fully in the body of the Speculum Vitae. Such repetition of subject matter is characteristic of the entire poem, as it is in a compendium adapted from a wide variety of related sources. A list of the topics included in Nassington's commentary on the Prologue in the First Exposition includes material mandated by the reform movement: The Ten Commandments (962-1213), the Twelve Articles of the Creed (1213-1265), the Seven Sacraments (1366-1407), the Seven Gifts of the Holy Spirit (1329-1362), the three Theological Virtues (1762-1868), and the four Cardinal Virtues (1870-2215).

>Pater (264-525)
>Nature of God as Alpha and Omega
>Free Will of mankind
>Attributes of the Father: might, wisdom, bounty
>Divine qualities of his children: nobleness, richness, beauty
>Virtues that make us like God: love, fear, obedience,
>   service, honor, reverence
>
>Noster (526-686)
>Grace adopting us as Sons of God
>Brotherhood as heirs with Christ
>Church as our Mother in the mystical Body
>Sins against the body of Christ: pride, hatred, avarice
>Hope of eternal unity with the Trinity
>
>Qui Es (687-1453)
>Inner life of the Trinity
>God as truth, steadfastness and eternity
>Difficulty of knowing and describing God
>Places where God is seen: Eucharist, hearts of holy men
>Attributes of the three persons of God: Might, Wisdom,
>   Bounty, Goodness
>Man's correspondence to the Trinity: Mind, Understanding, Will
>Indwelling of the Holy Spirit
>The Body as castle of God, with the senses as its gates
>The Church as truth of God

        Old Testament - 10 Commandments (962-1213)
        New Testament - 12 articles of Creed (1214-1328; 1407-1453)
        Grace through Gifts of Holy Spirit (1329-1362)
        7 Sacraments (1363-1406)

In Celis (1454-2293)
Omnipresence of God in heaven, earth, hearts of holy men
Heaven stirs us to see God's majesty
Way of perfection begins with penance and good works
Three conditions necessary for heaven:
    Meekness (1521-1761)
    Necessity of self-knowledge
    Foul condition of man
    Transitory nature of human life
    Thoughts on Christ's redemption
    Contrition: penance, prayer, conversion, confession
    Teaching as an expression of meekness

    Strength of Will (1762-2215)
    Theological Virtues
    Cardinal Virtues
    Virtues for right living
        Via activa
            Corporal Works of Mercy
            Spiritual Works of Mercy

        Via contemplativa
            Reading
            Thinking
            Praying

        Prowess (2219-2255)
        World
        Flesh
        Devil

    Conclusion (2256-2293)

Nassington concludes the Prologue by summarizing that Pater reveals the length of God's eternity, Noster reveals the breadth of his charity, Qui Es shows the depth of his fidelity, and In Celis reveals the height of God's majesty. Thus the First Exposition includes the required dogma of the reform movement and a plea urging the audience to begin the way of spiritual perfection.

It also points to Nassington's central doctrine on grace and the action of the Gifts of the Holy Spirit:

> Ys to trow in þe Haly Gaste,
> Þat is, to trow thurgh stedfastness
> Þat þe Haly Gaste suthfastely ys,
> Þe gyft and þe lufe of þe fader and þe son,
> As þai in hewyn to gedre won,
> Of wham comes alle goodes of grace
> In seven gyftys for to purchas,
> Þat for all our saules best shuld be,
> As ye salle after here and se (1331-39).

Second Exposition of the Petitions of the Pater Noster (2295-3306)

The Second Exposition contains the three elements common to all the Expositions: a call to pray the Pater Noster with a special faculty of the soul, a summary of the schema of Sevens, and an Exposition of the Seven Petitions. In the Second Exposition, Nassington pleads with his audience to pray the Pater Noster with "skylle," or reason, the faculty of the soul related to the Second Person of the Trinity, and proper to the soul progressing in perfection. As in the other commentaries, the Petitions are divided into two groups, the first three which center on spiritual concerns, and the second four which center on temporal matters:

> Of þes seven askynges, þe fyrst thre
> Makys a man here haly to be,
> And þe four þat after lys
> Make a man her right wys (2317-20).

The emphasis in the Second Exposition is on the key doctrine of grace in the <u>Speculum Vitae</u>, the action of the Gifts of the Holy Spirit, Nassington discusses the Gifts, one by one, in order of their importance to holiness, beginning with Wisdom and moving to Fear. He explains that the Gifts of the Holy Spirit are the essential divine action that impels growth in perfection because they draw out Vice and create a clean heart for the operation of Virtue. As he names each Petition of the Pater Noster, he presents a corresponding Gift of the Holy Spirit. This doctrine of the action of the Spirit is taken from St. Thomas' discussion of Gifts and Beatitudes in the second part of the Summa Theologiae. In presenting this complex doctrine, Nassington's language is more lyrical than in other doctrinal presentations.

The Second Exposition of the Pater Noster contains a second synopsis of the entire content of the Speculum Vitae, which stresses the action of the Gifts of the Spirit to advance in perfection:

> Aftir þat folous seven askynges
> Þat purchaces and tille us brynges
> Þe sevene gyfts of þe Haly Gast
> Þat to clene lyfying us may hast,
> Þe whilk out þe hert drawes
> Seven heved synnes þat with in grawes,
> And settys sevene maner of vertus
> In sted of þam þat men shuld us,
> Þe whilk a man evene ledys
> To sevne maner of blissed hedes (2307-2316)

This Second Exposition, which stresses the urgency of prayer, illustrates affective discourse. As Nassington develops his commentary on each Gift, he interposes a prayer, directly addressed to God the Father. He praises God for the action of the Gifts of the Holy Spirit experienced within his own soul, petitioning God that others may be grateful for supernatural grace. Thus, while the Second Exposition declares the mystery

of grace that draws souls to virtue, it does not conceal the
enthusiasm of Nassington as teacher for his subject matter.

Nassington introduces the Second Exposition with a prayer
of supplication addressed to the Lord, rather than to his
audience:

> Lord þis his our ȝernyng soverayn
> Over alle thynge, þus aske we,
> Þat halowed myght þe name be,
> Þat ys, þi knawyng and þi trouthe right
> Be festened in us day and nyght (2364-2368).

He urges his audience to taste and to savour the Gift of Divine
Wisdom, to experience the sweetness of God like "Gude likour and
fele./ By thy mouthe (2383-83)." Then he establishes his pattern
for the Second Exposition, elaborating on each petition:

> Þe name mot be halowed in us.
> Men shuld knawe and right hald
> Þat þis word þat haly is cald
> Ys as mekylle to say as clene
> As with outen erth to be seyn,
> As halowed to Goddys seruys,
> And to alle wekys þat bene rightwys
> As litted in blode ay to last
> As confermed and festened fast (2389-2397).

Nassington incorporates additional didactic material in the
Second Exposition, such as an instruction on the pious reception
of the Eucharist. An outline of the material illustrates his
emphasis on the action or working of the Gifts of the Holy Spirit.
After giving the relationship of each Petition to a Gift of the
Holy Spirit, Nassington's paraphrase exalts the benefits for the
soul conformed to the Imago Dei:

1. God is hallowed in the soul   (2294-2488)
Gift of Wisdom works three ways:
    a. Makes the heart holy
    b. Cleanses and refines the soul
    c. Draws the soul to the service of God
Baptism of blood in Christ
Description of the contemplative soul

> <u>Santificetur Nomen Tuum</u>
> Þat ys to say shortly þus
> Fader halow þi name in us,
> Þat er þi childern her thrugh skylle,
> Þat we do noȝt again þi wille,
> Bot þat we myght her in alle thynge
> Bouxsomly do alle þi bydyng   (2482-2488).

2. Kingdom of God within us   (2489-2597)
Gift of Understanding works to purify the heart of its murkiness
Description of God purifying the soul with a "sharp pyk"
Clearness of God's image in the holy soul
Joy of the holy soul turning from earth to heaven
Prayer of God to become master of the soul

> <u>Adveniat Regnum Tuum</u>
> Þat may be shortly sayd þus,
> Lord thurgh grace her regne in us
> Þat we thurgh blys may regne in þe
> In þe tothir werld þat ay shalle be,
> And þis same say we comonly
> For þam þat er in purgatory   (2591-2597).

3. God's will to be realized in us   (2598-2663).
Our will united to God like the angels'
Gift of Counsel works to help the Will govern the body

> <u>Fiat Voluntas Tua Sicut in Celo Et In Terra</u>
> Þat ys shortly þi wille be done
> In erth as ys in hewyn sone,
> Þat ys þus mekylle, for to say,
> Graunte us grace and myght here ay
> To do ay here with good talent
> Alle þat ys þi comandment,
> And þat þu for us byddes to leve it sone
> In earth as ys in hewyn done   (2629-2637).

Before continuing the Second Exposition, Nassington calls attention to the two divisions of Petitions, the three already discussed that are "Fulfylled in þe lyf þat ay salle last (2654)" and

the remaining four that meet needs "in þis lyf þat here ys sene
(2663)." The first three Petitions specify God's holiness,
kingdom and will. The final four petition God for earthly needs;
"Grant us, for gyf us, and kep us/ Delyver us (2658-59)."
Nassington continues to emphasize how the action and Gifts of the
Holy Spirit are linked to each petition:

    4.   Bread of the Eucharist (2664-2887)
    Gift of Strength to help us ask for needs
    Brotherhood especially in the religious life
    Instruction in the Eucharist

       <u>Panem Nostram Cotidianium Da Nobis Hodie</u>
       Þat may be sayd þus shortly and wele
       Grant us to day our bred to fele,
       Þat ys strenghte and heele namely,
       Bath of saule of body (2873-77).

   Summary: Bread for our bodies, wytt, and the Eucharist

    5.   Necessity of forgiveness (2888-3106)
    Court of Mercy as a tribunal of forgiveness
    Prayer with rancor is self-condemnation
    Commandment to love the image of God in enemies
    Gift of Knowledge works to seek forgiveness

       <u>Et Demitte Nobis Debita Nostra</u>
       Þat is to say on þis manere,
       Fader for gyf us our syn here
       Þat we have agayn þe wroght,
       In word, in dede, or in toght
       Right as we for gyf here wille
       To þem þat has done us ille (3101-3106).

    6.   Temptations of the world, flesh, devil (3107-3248)
    Tribulations as God's test of our love
    Foundation in Christ to resist temptation
    Gift of Piety works to strengthen the Will
    Grace is sufficient to avoid falling into temptation

       <u>Et Ne Nos Inducas In Temptacione</u>
       Þat ys to say þus shortly,
       Swet fadir Gode allemyghty
       Lede us noȝt in fondyng syn,

>   Þat ys, lat us noȝt entyr þar in
>   Thurgh wycked consentyng of herte
>   Or lyknge þat comes over thwert (3242-3247).

7. Asking for good keeps evil away
Relationship of sixth and seventh Petitions (3249-3277)
Gift of Fear works to help us avoid the perils of soul and body

>   <u>Sed Libera Nos A Malo</u>
>   Þat is to say fadir allemyghty
>   Delyvere us of alle ille haaly,
>   Þat ys of our faa þe fend,
>   And of his wyles þat may us shende,
>   Þat we thurghe pryd þa goddys noȝt tyne
>   Þay þu has gyffen us here of þine (3271-3277).

Conclusion (3277-3369)
Reminder of the gospel statement to ask and receive
Doxology of the Trinity
Right understanding of the Pater Noster
Reminder that God knows our needs better than we do
Prefer to pray for spiritual rather than bodily needs

Exactly how the prompting of the Holy Spirit moves human beings to virtuous actions is shown in Nassington's graphic illustration urging his audience to savor the gift of grace at work in the soul, an appeal directed to the uneducated:

>   Þan takys he a pyk sharp and smart
>   And grubbys and mynys about his hert
>   Ay tylle with in þe hert be
>   Þar he may alle his defautes se (2538-2541).

Nassington continues to explain the action of grace that finds sin, casts out "fylth," and makes the heart clean once more:

>   Bot when he has lang grubbyd about
>   Þan fyndes he in þe hert thurgh grace
>   Þees and rest, joy and solace (2557-2559).

Thus the soul is cleansed of its dimness so that it radiates the clear image of God. The soul is at rest in the peace of God; the supernatural goal of life is accomplished.

Third Exposition of the Petitions of the Pater Noster (3307-16,396)

Nassington begins the Third Exposition of the Petitions by recommending that the Pater Noster be prayed with the highest faculty of man, the Will. As the soul achieves perfection, the Will begins to comprehend the mysteries of God and to respond to them with love.

> Þarfor, when we salle to Gode pray
> Þe hert behoues thynk and þe tong say
> So þat tonge þe hert ay fele,
> And with þe hert acord wele (3341-42).

The Third Exposition introduces the entire pentad of Sevens: the Petitions of the Pater Noster, Gifts of the Holy Spirit, Vice, Virtues and Beatitudes. As in the other introductory commentaries, the Third Exposition also includes a summary of the body of the Speculum Vitae:

> Þis þrayer þat pus falles to begyne
> Has sevene sikere askyngs with in,
> As ȝe have herd me befor telle,
> And mare wille say if ȝe wille dwelle
> Þes sevene us wynnes and makys us tast
> Þe sevene gyftys of þe Haly Gast,
> And puttes out of þe hert evene
> Þe pricipalle dedly synnes sevene
> With alle par branches pat may be sene,
> And makys þe hert of alle synnes clene,
> And in þar stede with in setts right
> Sevene maner of vertuous of myght,
> The whilk vertus a man right ledys
> Untille þe sevene blyssed hedys,
> And to sevene medys þat to þam lyse
> As I shalle shew on sere wyse (3370-3381)

New to the Third Exposition are the specific Vices, Virtues, and Beatitudes that are connected to each Petition of the Pater Noster. They are part of the doctrine legislated by the church Councils, which provides the structural frame for the body of the <u>Speculum Vitae</u>. The Gifts of the Holy Spirit have "sere offices" (3631) to dispel Vice and implant Virtue. Before the long commentaries on each Vice and Virtue, Nassington shows the inter-relatedness of his entire schema, giving a brief overview of each petition (3307-3506). For example, perfection begins with the action of the Gift of Fear. Fear "puttes and settys/meknes (3495-3496)," and Meekness will "lighty lede (3497)" to the blessedness of heavenly perfection and its reward. Throughout the commentary, Nassington demonstrates that the Gift "puttes," or "drawes out" Vice, which "settes" Virtue in place, and "bringes" or "ledys" the Christian to the Beatitude. Thus he communicates to a learned and lewd audience the complex doctrine of the action of grace through the Gifts of the Holy Spirit as initially formulated in the <u>Summa Theologiae</u> by St. Thomas.

Nassington explains that grace, empowering the soul to achieve perfection, operates through a series of seven pentads, each identified with a Petition of the Pater Noster. The summary at the beginning of the Third Exposition specifies this content (3385-3498):

First Petition	Hallowed be thy name
Gift	Wisdom
Vice	Gluttony
Virtue	Soberness
Beatitude	Blessed are the peacemakers
	They shall be called sons of God
Second Petition	Thy kingdom come
Gift	Understanding
Vice	Lechery
Virtue	Chastity
Beatitude	Blessed are the clean of heart
	They shall see God
Third Petition	Thy will be done
Gift	Counsel
Vice	Avarice
Virtue	Mercy
Beatitude	Blessed are the merciful
	They shall have mercy
Fourth Petition	Give us our daily bread
Gift	Strength
Vice	Sloth
Virtue	Prowess
Beatitude	Blessed are those who hunger and thirst for righteousness
	They shall be filled
Fifth Petition	Forgive us our debts
Gift	Knowledge
Vice	Wrath
Virtue	Evenhead (Equity)
Beatitude	Blessed are the sorrowful
	They shall be comforted
Sixth Petition	Lead us not into temptation
Gift	Piety
Vice	Envy
Virtue	Friendship
Beatitude	Blessed are the meek
	They shall inherit the land
Seventh Petition	Deliver us from evil
Gift	Fear
Vice	Pride
Virtue	Meekness
Beatitude	Blessed are the poor in spirit
	Theirs is the kingdom of heaven

After this overview of the content in the Third Exposition, Nassington begins his long commentary on each Petition (3507-16,396). Here the order of Petitions is reversed from the usual sequence of the Pater Noster. Basing his argument on the prophet David's declaration that the Fear of the Lord is the beginning of Wisdom, Nassington holds that perfection begins with the Gift of Fear which casts out Pride, the root of all sin. Accordingly, instruction in spiritual growth must begin with the action of the Gift of Fear, and move to the Gift of Wisdom. This is the subject matter of the Seventh Petition of the Pater Noster. Thus, the detailed explication of the Third Exposition begins with the last Petition, "Deliver us from evil," and its corresponding Gift, Vice, Virtue, and Beatitude.

Whereas the Third Exposition of the Petitions appears to be a tidy schema of Sevens, Nassington's treatment of individual topics is extraordinarily diverse. This chart, on page 97, indicates the irregular number of lines given to each topic, and shows Nassington's emphasis on the three Petitions calling for spiritual goods. They are linked with the intellectual Gifts, those that perfect the mystical life. As explained by Thomas, Wisdom and Understanding perfect mankind for the contemplative life, while Piety and Fortitude, for example, perfect mankind for the active life. Thus, two-thirds of the text of the Speculum Vitae concerns the perfection of the unitive way, which is discussed in Chapter IV.

On the other hand, this outline does not represent the Third Exposition of the Petitions of the Pater Noster accurately. Many

	Gifts	Vices	Virtues	Blessing/Reward	
Deliver us from evil	Fear 133	Pride 251	Humility 297	Poor/kingdom of heaven	17
Forgive us our debts	Piety 16	Envy 201	Friendship 179	Meek/inherit the land	19
Lead us not into temptation	Knowledge 48	Wrath 77	Evenhead 193	Mourn/be comforted	15
Give us our daily bread	Fortitude 13	Sloth 293	Prowess 823	Righteous/be filled	19
Your will be done	Counsel 9	Avarice 1498	Mercy 1655	Mercy/mercy	109
Your kingdom come	Understanding 37	Lechery 361	Chastity 3430	Clean of heart/see God	13
Hallowed be your name	Wisdom 264	Gluttony 1651	Soberness 1118	Peacemakers/Sons of God	13

of the subjects named in my chart of the Speculum Vitae have been
treated in earlier sections. Each of the two introductory
Expositions includes a paraphrase of each Petition, and the Second
Exposition elaborates on the Gifts of the Holy Spirit. Some of the
Virtues, too, are mentioned in the Introduction: Strength as
related to Strength of Will (1762-2215), the intellectual Gifts of
Wisdom (2369-2470), Understanding (2502-2517), and Counsel (2261-2635)
in the Prologue. The Vices of Pride and Avarice (634-665) are also
treated in the Prologue.

Furthermore, the outline indicates that only a few lines are
devoted to each Beatitude, which is not representative of their
centrality as the goal of perfection. The meaning of four of the
Beatitudes is explained at a point where it is related to other
topics. Meekness, named as the Second Beatitude, is extensively
developed in the Prologue (1520-2555). Nassington's commentary
on the Virtue of Evenness (4715-4748) and the Virtue of Prowess
(5271-6094) in the Third Exposition explicates the Third and Fourth
Beatitudes. The Fifth Beatitude, Blessed are the merciful, is
included under the "Third Asking" in the commentary on the
Spiritual (7838-8265) and Corporal (8266-8825) Works of Mercy.

Moreover, the meaning of the Beatitudes pervades the entire
Speculum Vitae, reflecting Nassington's debt to Augustine's
De sermone in monte. In that work Augustine teaches that the
counsels of Christ are a rule of life for all his followers. He
compares Christ as law giver, promulgating the New Law, to Moses
as legislator of the Commandments of the Old Law on Mount Sinai.

Augustine reduces Matthew's eight Beatitudes to seven, noting that since the first and eighth both mention the kingdom of God as the reward, they can be conflated. For Augustine, the seven Beatitudes specify the stages leading to contemplation. He compares the seven Beatitudes with the seven Gifts of the Holy Spirit, seeing in them a corresponding ascent to truth. Wisdom, the contemplation of truth which draws humankind to the likeness of God, is the highest stage in perfection. The Augustinian schema, expanded from the fourth century, is the structural framework for Nassington's theology on the Beatitudes:

Beatitudes	Gifts of the Holy Spirit
1. Humility	Fear of the Lord
2. Meekness	Godliness
3. Sorrow	Knowledge
4. Justice	Fortitude
5. Mercy	Counsel
6. Purity	Understanding
7. Peace	Wisdom[6]

The correspondence between each pair of Beatitudes and Gifts evolves from the doctrine of the patristic writers that the New Law is an internal law, that is, the presence of the Holy Spirit in the human heart. For Augustine, and later Irenaeus, the New Law as it is represented in the Beatitudes is the living force of the Holy Spirit, infusing grace which teaches and sanctifies the Christian by love.

In addition to the subjects called for by the reform movement -- the Pater Noster Petitions, Gifts of the Holy Spirit, Vices, Virtues and Beatitudes -- Nassington incorporates other didactic material into the Third Exposition. His topics, their divisions and sub-divisions, are allied with contemporaneous treatises on the Vices and Virtues, such as the <u>Somme le Roi</u> and the <u>Prick of Conscience</u>. Nassington follows the medieval practice referring to each Petition as an "Asking."

<u>Seventh Asking</u>   (3507-4205)

    Gift of Fear
    Vice of Pride
    7 roots of Pride, many branches
    Virtue of Meekness
    7 degrees of Meekness
    7 branches of Meekness
    Beatitude of spiritual poverty

<u>Sixth Asking</u>   (4206-4624)

    Gift of Pity
    Vice of Envy
    3 parts of Envy
    6 sins against the Holy Spirit
    Virtue of Friendship
    7 degrees of Friendship
    7 branches of Friendship
    Gift of Piety working in the mystical Body
    Beatitude of Meekness

<u>Fifth Asking</u>   (4625-4962)

    Gift of Knowing
    Vice of Wrath
    4 kinds of Wrath
    7 ways Wrath spreads
    Virtue of Evenhead
    Evenhead accords Reason and Will
    4 kinds of Evenhead in Reason
    4 kinds of Evenhead in Will
    7 degrees of Evenhead
    7 branches of Evenhead to oppose 7 deadly sins
    Gift of knowing (second discussion)
    6 manners of greeting
    Beatitude of Comfort

<u>Fourth Asking</u>   (4963-6114)

    Gift of Strength
    Vice of Sloth
    6 ways to bring us to good amendment

6 deterrents to amendment of heart
6 ways to bring us to an ill ending
Virtue of Prowess
6 branches or battles of prowess
6 conditions for confession
6 requirements for repentance
5 sins set in the heart by the fiend
Satisfaction for sin
Beatitude of Righteousness

Third Asking   (6115-9379)

Gift of Counsel
Vice of Avarice
3 ways Avarice shows
10 branches of the tree of Avarice
Virtue of Mercy
7 degrees of the tree of Mercy
7 branches of Mercy, the spiritual works of Mercy
7 branches of Mercy, the corporal works of Mercy
3 in almsgiving
Fruit of Mercy
Beatitude of Mercy

Second Asking   (9380-13,224)

Gift of Understanding
3 benefits of Understanding
Vice of Lechery
4 kinds of temptation to Lechery
4 divisions of Lechery of heart
14 divisions of Lechery of body
Virtue of Chastity
7 degrees of the tree of Chastity
4 pillars of devout prayer
7 states of Chastity
3 sins against the white robe of Virginity
6 leaves of Chastity
3 grains of the lily of Chastity
Beatitude to see God

First Asking   (13,225-16,395)

Gift of Wisdom
Vice of Gluttony
Dialogue with the belly
5 branches of Gluttony
10 branches of the idle tongue
Gift of Wisdom   (second discussion)
Virtue of Soberness

>   3 goods to Soberness
>   3 helps to Soberness
>   3 benefits of Soberness
>   7 degrees of Soberness
>   2 fruits of Soberness
>   Beatitude to become Sons of God

What appears to be a pedantic categorization of religious material is made lively by Nassington's illustrations from the Old and New Testament and from contemporary life in England. He provides vivid illustrations of his topics from Scripture, such as the classic example of Lucifer to exemplify Pride, Mary Magdalene to represent Contrition, and the crucified Christ to demonstrate Meekness. Nassington's citations show his love for authorities, such as Ambrose, Anselm, Gregory, Cyprian and Augustine. Other elements from religious writing include the Pauline image of the Christian warrior, Prudentius <u>Psychomachia</u>, and the metaphor of the body as a castle, seen in the <u>Ancrene Riwle</u>, Grosseteste's <u>Le Chateau d'Amour</u>, and the <u>Templum Domini</u>. He also employs the device of the tree of Vices and Virtues and the metaphor of grace as a medicinal restorative for the sick soul, both found in Grosseteste's <u>Templum Domini</u>. The quotation from the pagan philosopher, Seneca, and the allusion to the historical King Alexander confirm Nassington's wide range of knowledge. Nonetheless, two traditional images, the <u>Speculum</u> and the stairway to the mountain of perfection, dominate the <u>Speculum Vitae</u>.

Nassington's Narration on the Vice of Avarice

The treatment of the Vice of Avarice is one of the most convincing arguments for Nassington's authorship of the <u>Speculum Vitae</u>.

He draws from his experience as a medieval ecclesiastic for examples of Avarice and its ten Branches. Here his former reliance on authorities shown in statements such as "As the bok appertly says," "as synt Paul in a bok shewys," or "in the gospelle þat soth ys," disappears. Instead Nassington speaks from his own authority, claiming "as I wene," and "as I undirstand," or instructing "Bot he do I warn him wele." In his section on Avarice (6125-7623) and to some extent in his discussion of Hypocrisy, a division of Gluttony (13,403-13,779), Nassington's narrative voice is heard recounting experience, passing judgment, delivering polemics, and issuing exhortations against the evil of Avarice.

Nassington emerges as a staunch proponent of civil and ecclesiastical morality in this section. His illustration of the privy thief, who steals goods and keeps them, is followed by his warning concerning the final judgment:

> Fra Gode may noȝt þat theif be hyde,
> And if he scape here þe lawe of land
> To Goddys lawe byhoves hym stande,
> For when his saule ys hyns femyd,
> Thurghe Goddys lawe he salle be demyd
> And perchance to endeles payn,
> Bot if he ȝeld it here agayn (6371-6376).

Likewise, Nassington passes judgment on the covert thief, who surreptitiously steals his master's goods:

> So sleghtly stelys he his lord rent
> Me thynk he war worthy to be shent (6387-6388).

He issues a warning to the "lyttle thief," the servant who takes a few hens or such small store from his master:

>   And bot he do I warn hym wele
>   Fulle hard payn þan salle he fele,
>   Þat lastys perchance with outyn ende
>   When he out of þis world shalle wende (6441-6444).

Nassington rules that even the bailiff who aborts justice by accepting a bribe is guilty of felony, for he is assenting to theft (6467-6502).

Nassington provides graphic examples of each of these divisions of "chalange," a section of Avarice pertaining to false claims in court: false plaintiff, false defendant, false witness and false reporter of inquest, false advocate or pleader, false procurator and attorney, false notary, and false justice and judge. He would suspend the notary who falsifies a document:

>   Bot if he attaynt ware of þat wyce
>   He shulde be suspent of his offyce;
>   Or he þat clerkys ys of þe croune,
>   Of kynges court of or court baroun,
>   Þat makys any fals recorde
>   Or falschede duse untille his lorde,
>   Shewys his counsaille or falses his seel,
>   Or ȝit his lordys avantage stele,
>   Me thynke he ware worthy bedrawen.
>   As a traytoure if war knawen,
>   And sithen be hanged by þe hals
>   If þat he ware attenyd so fals,
>   Bot alle if he skep þe payn here,
>   His saule mone by þat falshed dere (7003-7016).

While these passages demonstrate Nassington's knowledge of English common law, he speaks with similar authority on matters pertaining to canon law. His illustration of simony presents the unethical transference of a benefice:

>   Anothir ys þat I fynde a vyce
>   Þat ys gyft of benyfyce,
>   For he þat may a benefyce gyf
>   On whilk a clerk may goodly lyf,
>   Kyrk prebend or vicary,
>   Fre chapelle or chauncery,
>   He thynks noȝt gyf hym mast,

>   Or to hym to whome he dete owe,
>   Or for the frenship of some felowe,
>   Or for othir cause þay mat be,
>   And noȝt anely for charyte (7179-7190).

The improper procurement of a religious office is another type of simony:

>   Þe fourt may in eleccioun be
>   Of prelacy or of dygnyte,
>   For when a colage or a convent,
>   Salle chese a prelate thurgh assent
>   To dignyte or to prelacy,
>   Þai chese ane þat ys unworthy;
>   In eleccioun þai accord
>   Thurgh prayer or procurment of lord.
>   Þus er chosen thurgh swylk favour
>   Bath bishopp, abbott, and pryore,
>   Þarfor, thurgh swylk eleccioun
>   Ye haly kyrk nere hand broght done (7199-7210).

Nassington's harshest judgment is against those who exchange the word of God for worldly goods:

>   I hald þat prechoure nerehand wode
>   Þat sellys Goddys word for warldly goode,
>   Or he þat prest ys and wille noȝt
>   Syng a messe bot it be boght.
>   Or wille noȝt here a mans shryft,
>   Ne housylle hum bot he have gyft,
>   Or oght takys by þat entente
>   For any oder sacrymente
>   Na better may he þan be cald
>   Þan Judas was þat Cryst sald (7237-7246).

He condemns clergy who gamble or use the church for gaming, practicing "fole play," the tenth Branch of Avarice. Nassington's denouncement of corrupt clerics, demanding reform, recalls Richard Rolle's polemics against clerical corruption:

>   Ille ensampille, me thynk, þai gyf
>   To othir men þat wele shuld lyf (7588-7589).
>
>   Ȝit me thynk unbouxsom er þai
>   To haly kyrk þat uses þat play,
>   For haly kyrk defendys swylk werkys

>   And namely to prestys and clerkys,
>   Alle þase þat duse pair agayn
>   Shuld be chasted thurgh þair soverayne (7606-7611)

A comparison of Nassington's treatment of Avarice with that of the <u>Somme le Roi</u> verifies that he adapted traditional material. Lorens' <u>Somme le Roi</u> lists three Branches and ten boughs of Avarice; Nassington presents Ten Branches of Avarice. Lorens lists seven types of Usury; Nassington discusses twelve. The <u>Somme le Roi</u> lists seven kinds of "chalenge"; Nassington cites eight.

Nassington's variations are most evident in his original examples for the Vice of Avarice. The <u>Somme le Roi</u> includes only two specific illustrations: the knight who incurred God's vengeance by blasphemy, and the archer who attempted to spite God by shooting an arrow upward. Nassington's long treatment of Avarice abounds in illustrative cases drawn from his experience as a canon and a cleric.

Nassington received his apprenticeship as canon under John de Grandisson, appointed as Bishop of Exeter in 1327 at a time when the bishopric was in debt and the cathedral needed rebuilding. At the same time, the Papacy placed monetary demands upon the diocese. Grandisson, an heir to family wealth, was a substantial benefactor of his new diocese, and consonant with his own generosity, asked his clergy, abbots, and priors to make contributions. F. C. Hingeston-Randolph, editor of the <u>Register of Grandisson</u>, suggests that Grandisson may have been the first bishop to send out a diocesan-wide financial appeal.[7] Bishop Grandisson's efforts to solicit money were rebuffed by his own religious, neighboring prelates, and secular magnates, who apparently saw him as a formidable rival.

While Grandisson attended to his duties at the see in Exeter, he sent Nassington as his representative to raise money throughout the diocese and to negotiate financial settlements in Grandisson's place. Nassington was compelled to arbitrate Grandisson's demands, which are called "excessivo," and "persolvendo" in the letters preserved in the Register of Grandisson. For his effort to resolve Exeter's financial crisis, Grandisson describes Nassington as his eager assistant, "fervidam invenimus assistricem." This early canonical experience introduced Nassington to the evil practice of Avarice. In a similar way, his position as deputy necessitated adjudicating disputes in religious houses, such as the case of the improper election procedure which Nassington uses to illustrate a Branch of Simony (7179-7190). The records of Nassington's activity in Exeter and in York as "official" and "visitor" resound in the Speculum Vitae as vivid illustrations of the Vice of Avarice.

NOTES

[1] W. A. Pantin, *The English Church in the Fourteenth Century* (Cambridge: University Press, 1955), p. 228.

[2] St. Thomas Aquinas, *Summa Theologiae*, Vol. 24, *The Gifts of the Spirit* (1a2ae. 68-70), Edward C. O'Connor, trans. (New York: McGraw-Hill, 1973), p. xvi.

[3] J. E. Wells, *A Manual of the Writings in Middle English* 1050-1400 (New Haven: Yale University Press, 1916), gives 1350 for the earliest version of *Octovan*, 118; 1350-1400 for the composition of *Sir Isumbras*, 114; the English *Bevis of Hamptoun* about 1300, 21; and the English *Guy of Warwick* in the Auchinleck manuscript c. 1330-1340, p. 16.

[4] A. I. Doyle, "A Survey of the Origins and Circulation of Theological Writings in English in the 14th, 15th and early 16th Centuries," Diss. Downing College, 1953, p. 63.

[5] Doyle, p. 331, n. 10.

[6] John J. Jepsen, trans., *St. Augustine: The Lord's Sermon on the Mount* (Westminster, Maryland; Newman Press, 1948), p. 7. The introduction including this schema was prepared by the editors, Johannes Quaesten and Joseph C. Plumpe.

[7] *The Register of John de Grandisson, Bishop of Exeter*, 1327-1369 (London: George Bell, 1899), Pt. I, Preface, p. xv.

CHAPTER IV

THE SPECULUM VITAE AS A MANUAL OF PERFECTION

The catechetical doctrine described in Chapter Three justifies reading the *Speculum Vitae* as a mystical treatise in which Nassington describes the three traditional stages of Purgation (incipientes), Illumination (proficientes), and Union (perfecti). Characterizing the development of any life cycle, they are applied to the supernatural life of God in the soul as birth, growth, and fulfillment or perfection. This chapter will show how the three Expositions of the *Speculum Vitae* are linked to the progressive stages in the way of perfection, while the Seven Petitions of the Pater Noster with their corresponding Vices and Virtues are allied with different types of prayer:

<u>Purgation</u> - Discursive prayer

1. Deliver us from evil   Pride   Meekness
2. Lead us not into temptation   Envy   Friendship
3. Forgive us our sins   Wrath   Evenhead
4. Give us our daily bread   Sloth   Prowess

<u>Illumination</u> - Affective meditation

5. Thy will be done   Avarice   Mercy
6. Thy kingdom come   Lechery   Chastity

<u>Mystical Union</u> - Contemplation

7. Hallowed be thy name   Gluttony   Soberness

Each Exposition is linked to a separate faculty which fosters a different type of prayer: understanding is appropriate for discursive prayer, reason promotes for affective meditation, and the will brings the soul to mystical union.

Each stage of the mystical life has a proper work which is accomplished through different elements of the pentad of sevens. Purgation uproots Vice through the Petitions, Illumination brings Virtue through the Gifts of the Holy Spirit, and Mystical Union culminates in the Beatitudes. Thus the schema of the <u>Speculum Vitae</u> encompasses the <u>via mystica</u>. The process of purgation strips the soul of selfishness through penance, mortification, and the practice of good works; illumination restores the <u>Imago Dei</u> to the soul, attaching it to spiritual goods; and mystical union perfects the soul through contemplation, directing it to social action. The First and Second Expositions introduce the central aspects of Purgation and Illumination, while the Third Exposition provides a detailed treatment of the entire process leading to mystical union.

The ultimate goal of perfection is to restore the image of the Trinitarian God in the <u>speculum</u> of the soul. First, Nassington establishes the correspondence between the mystery of the Trinity and the nature of the human soul. The presence of the Trinity as revealed by faith includes three Persons: the Father who begets the Son, who loves the Father with the same infinite love with which the Father loves Him; out of this mutual love proceeds the Holy Spirit, a person equal to the Father and Son, and a mutual bond between them. As an image of the Trinitarian God, each human being is endowed with the faculty of Reason which begets Understanding, resulting in Love, or the faculty of the Will. A specific attribute is given to each person in the Trinity:

>   And to þes tre, thre things falles:
>   Vn to the fader fyrst falles myght,
>   And to þe son falles wysdome right,
>   And to þe Haly Gast gudnes (865-868).

Divine Might, Wisdom, and Goodness, in turn, correspond to the human faculties of Mind, Understanding, and Will (869-892). Since God is mirrored in the soul through the human faculties, it is possible for mankind, strengthened by grace, to restore the *Imago Dei* to the soul:

>   For why alle þe halynes of a man,
>   As þes clerks shew vs cane,
>   þat is mad right lyk to be
>   To þe ymage of þe trynite
>   After thre thynges þat er sene
>   In þe saule þat þes thre bene:
>   Mynd, Vndirstandyng, and wille,
>   þat ys in þes thre thynges thurgh skylle
>   In þat at þe saule in þe body
>   Be clensed in the wille perfitely
>   Of alle kyn maner of fyllyng,
>   And lyghtend wele in þe vndirstandyng,
>   And perfytely conformed in þe mynde
>   In Gode and with Gode þat tok man kynd;
>   And þe more largely þat þe saul fre
>   Resavues of Gode þes gyftes thre
>   þe mare properly it neghes nere
>   To his kynd beute þat ys clere,
>   þat ys of þe bounte þat comes mast
>   Of the fadir, and þe son, and þe haly gast;
>   þay ys when Gode þi fader fre
>   Conformes in mans hert mynd to be,

> Gode þe son with outen lettyng
> Lyghtens his vndirstandyng,
> And Gode þe Haly Gast to fele
> His wille at þe last clenses wele;   (2321-2346).

Nassington draws from traditional sources on Trinitarian exemplarism to develop his position. Eric Colledge traces the development of the <u>Imago Dei</u> from the patristic fathers to the Middle Ages, recounting how Augustine derived the concept of the <u>regio dissimilitudinis</u> from Plotinus, the Platonist, who adapted it from Plato who wrote that God's guidance was needed if the earth was not to plunge into the "region of unlikeness."[1] Plotinus taught that the lapsed soul must travel from sin through virtue toward God through its likeness to him. Augustine clarified that the soul was God's image through reason and his likeness through intelligence.[2] Anselm of Canterbury, using Augustine's comparison of the soul to a coin, stamped with a representation of its maker that disappears as it becomes worn down, claimed that the soul's image of God was worn away by the friction of vices.[3] Bede borrowed Augustine's image and with Anselm propagated "image theology" in England. Nassington's contemporary, Walter Hilton, adapted the same teaching in the <u>Scale of Perfection</u>, naming Anselm's friction of vices the <u>Imago Peccati</u>.[4] In drawing on this tradition of Trinitarian exemplarism, Nassington posits that the Gifts of the Holy Spirit are the action of grace that

obliterates the Imago Peccati and restores the Imago Dei to
the soul:

> þe haly gyft of vndirstandyng
> þat may a man to clene lyf brynge,
> For as the son puttes a way
> In myrknes of þe nyght and maks þe day,
> And wastes þe cloudes þat myrk bene,
> And þe mornyng mystes þat er sene
> Right so þis gyft þat men tastes
> Alle þe myrknes of þe hert wastes
> And shewys his syn thurgh clernes,
> And alle his defautes mare and les,
> So þat he þat wenes, he ys clene,
> Salle fynd in þe hert, as I wene,
> To mekylle poudre þar in dwelle
> Of syn with outen nowmber to telle
> As þe sone beme shewys right
> Poudre and motes þer it shynes bright (2502-2517).

To restore the Imago Dei to the soul, the Three Expositions outline the via mystica as a progressive journey, prompted by the Gifts of the Holy Spirit and built upon a structure of seven steps.

The Beginning Process of Purgation

Nassington introduces the process of Purgation in the First Exposition (98-2294), elaborating upon the elements in the body of the Speculum Vitae. Built upon the petitions of the Pater Noster concerning temporal goods, spiritual advancement begins with knowledge of self (205-242). The beginner in the spiritual life seeks forgiveness for sin and freedom from temptation and evil, whereas more advanced souls seek spiritual goods: a steadfast will, the kingdom of God, and the grace of eternal happiness. Achieving union with God is a gradual climb beginning with the exercises of Purgation:

>   And who so ӡernys to come so heghe
>   Hym be houes clymb vp by a steghe
>   þat shuld be made, as says þes clerks,
>   Of hard penannce, and haly werrks;
>   For þider comes na man to hym,
>   Bot he wille by þis steghe clymbe,
>   Bot who so wille his syn for sayk
>   Bygnnes þan þis stegh to mayke;
>   And þam þat of na penannce irkys,
>   Ne almus dede þis steghe wyrkys (1510-1519).

The three virtues Nassington names to begin this arduous task are meekness, strength of will, and "pruesce of hert," or perseverence. Meekness includes thinking, contrition, suffering, and holy delight (1526-1760). The beginner considers how he is conceived in orginal sin and lives in a murky, earthly valley as a pilgrim on his way to the final judgment. He reflects that he is made in God's image, redeemed through Christ's Passion and Death, and brought to contrition, penance and prayer. The second essential virtue, strength of will, embraces the three theological virtues of faith, hope, and charity (1726-2215). Drawing from St. Paul, Nassington argues that the greatest of these is charity:

>   For he þat lufs nogt with hert fre
>   His brother when he ay may se,
>   How shuld he luf in hert right
>   Gode of wham he has no syght (1842-1845).

The four cardinal virtues, named by Solomon in the Book of Wisdom, and another aspect of strength of will, aid the beginner to act with reason, to bridle the will, to resist temptation, and to practice charity (1870-2149). The third virtue, "pruesce," helps the beginner to overcome the world, the flesh, and the devil and thereby to earn a crown of everlasting life (2216-2225).

Accordingly, self-knowledge brings the beginner to recognize his sinfulness, to practice penance, and to desire to know God in prayer and to serve Him through others in the body of the Church. The way of perfection may be pursued through the active life (2150-2171) or the contemplative life (2174-2215). The first four Petitions, concerning temporal goods, are directed primarily toward those in the active life, whereas the three Petitions naming spiritual goods are directed to contemplatives. As Nassington elaborates on the steps to perfection in the Third Exposition, he follows the schema explained in Chapter Three, so that each step links a Petition to a Gift, a process which eradicates a Vice, implants a Virtue, and leads to a Beatitude.

For example, Nassington's explication of the first step of purgation illustrates how Fear uproots Pride with Meekness. Pride is remedied as one acknowledges his dependence upon God for all good (3641-3892). This dependence is spiritual poverty, the blessing named in the first Beatitude (4191-4205). Meekness counters Pride through self-effacement, causing the soul to know and act upon its truth, thus opening the way for grace (3893-4205). The beginner must first destroy Pride with its seven roots:

>   þe furst rote þar wrytyn ys
>   Ys properly vnfaithfulnes,
>   þe secunde ys dispite þar by,
>   þe thyrde men calles surquydry,
>   þe fourt ys, as clerkys wate,

>   Couatyng of highe state,
>   þe fyft men calles wayn glory,
>   And þe sext ipocrycy,
>   þe seuents us fole shame to hyde (3643-3651).

The fifth root of Pride, vainglory, demonstrates how easily one becomes a victim of Pride's deception:

>   þe fende bycomes a marchand,
>   þat he haldys his mone of prys
>   Thurgh whilk he makys his marchandys,
>   He wendes about on ilk a syde
>   Thurgh the fayr of þis werld wyde (3802-3806).

Pride's inordinate self-love is uprooted through a series of spiritual exercises, described by Nassington as degrees of meekness:

>   Ane ys to honor Gode anely
>   Both with hert and with body,
>   Another ys to prays ilk man,
>   þe third ys to lake our self þan,
>   þe fourt ys to luf pouert by skylle,
>   þe fyft ys to serue with god wille,
>   þe sext to fle of alle losse þe cry,
>   þe seuent to traist in Gode anely (3951-3958).

Christ is an exemplar of meekness, retreating to a mountain to pray in absolute dependency upon His Father. In imitation of Christ, the beginner comprehends the transitory nature of the world in such moments of solitary prayer:

>   And hi ys rauyshede to hewyn so heghe,
>   þan seys he þe werld lytylle þat tyde
>   Unto þe regarde of hewyn so wyde,
>   He seys it foule thurghe þe ayere
>   Vnto þe regarde of hewyn so fayre,
>   Fulle vgly it semys tille his sight
>   As to regarde of hewyn so bright,
>   And alle woyd semys þe world to be
>   As to regarde of grete plente,
>   þat he þan seys in hewyn ryke
>   Of alle kyn good þat þe hert may lyk,

>þan begynnes he þe world dispyse
>For hym thynk it noȝt bot fantyse (4166-4178).

In the second step of Purgation, Envy, which stirs hatred, sows discord, and fosters an inordinate desire for riches and honor, is uprooted by Friendship, through which all persons are seen as the Body of Christ. Envy is the Vice most despised by God, for it includes the sins against the Holy Spirit, sins that are seldom confessed or forgiven (4223-4280).

>Ane ys presumpcion of herte bald
>þat ys our hopp in ynglych tald,
>Wanehope ys þe secund syne
>Wa ys hym þat endys þar in,
>þe third ys herdnes of herte,
>þe fourt ys dispice of penance smert,
>þe fyft ys wreynge in othir men
>Of þe grace of Haly Gast to ken
>þe sext syn þat after ys
>Werrynge agayn suthfastness (4341-4350).

Friendship with its seven degrees is grounded in the unity of faith, God's Fatherhood, and the church with its Sacraments (4425-4604). As Friendship destroys selfishness which breeds Envy, the beginner extends charity to others.

In the third step of Purgation, Wrath, the irrational passion, is tempered by Evenhead, or Equity, which brings reason and will into accord (4715-4908). Wrath is spread in seven different ways:

>Ane ys schryft thurgh wordes smerte,
>Ane othir ys rancor in hert,
>þe third ys hatred pryue,
>þe fourt may wele be cald medle,
>þe fyft ys ernyng of wengange,
>þe sext ys sclaghter thurgh myschaunce,
>þe seuent ys were þat þan falles sone,
>Thurgh whilk many men er for done (4681-4688).

Reason brings the soul to form a right conscience, a gradual process described by Nassington as manners of "clere sight (4769-4872)." To help form the conscience, Nassington provides a detailed examination of the will, five senses, worldly attachments, companions, and actions. As the beginner chooses good and becomes aware of evil not chosen, he sorrows for the sin of the world. Thus the soul mourns for all who commit the seven deadly sins (4873-4908), which corresponds to the Third Beatitude.

In the final step of purgation, Sloth, causing the soul to be negligent in performing spiritual exercises, is uprooted by Prowess, strengthening the soul in virtue. Sloth is eradicated by a discipline of the will against indifference and of the body against laziness (4977-5270). The devil tempts the slothful through procrastination, spiritual blindness, cowardliness, and faint-heartedness. Nassington demonstrates how the devil persuades the soul, delaying his spiritual progress:

> For þu ert ȝounge and haale of hert,
> And þu semys stalward man and smert,
> Bath to ryde and to gange
> And be ȝou siker þu salle lyf lange,
> Sen þu of lyf has lange space
> Whils þu ert ȝong tak þi solace (5119-5124).

"Pruesce," a virtue "þat makys a man hardy and wyse (5272)", and its seven degrees replaces Sloth (5271-5396). The last degree of prowess names the Fourth Beatitude:

> Nobylnes of hert in ilk a chance,
> Trustyng, sikernes, and suffirance,
> Stedfastne þat meklle may a waille,

> And lastandnes with outyn faille,
> Hungre and thryst of rightwysnes,
> And ilkane of þes a vertue ys (5279-5284).

As the soul advances, God arms it, protects it, and guides it through the battles against the seven deadly sins, leading it to the crown of everlasting life (5397-6094):

> þe furst bataylle to be gyne
> Ys þe bataylle of dedely syne,
> Anothir ys of pennance harde,
> þe third ys of þe flesshe so fraward,
> þe fourt and þe fygt of þe world er twa
> þe tane of welth, þe tothir of wa,
> þe sext of wyched men and fele,
> And þe seuente of þe fende of hele (5407-5414).

Because these battles of Prowess are won through confession, penance, and amendment, Nassington includes another examen, enumerating sins of thought, word, deed, and omission (5590-5838). But God is faithful to the soul, especially in the trials against riches and honor:

> þe fourt and þe fyft bataylle þan
> þe world brynges to assaile a man,
> And dame fortune with hir whele
> þat turnes about, as man may fele,
> þe world, a man her assayles
> On aythir syd with two batayles
> þe ta bataylle ys, as I gesce,
> Of honors, delyces, and rychesce (5973-5978, 5981-82).

Despite the efforts of the beginner to eradicate vice, the enemies of the spirit -- the world, the flesh, and the devil -- besiege the soul with temptation. God permits this as a greater means of meriting heaven, for the more the soul merits his everlasting reward, the greater shall be his joy and honor. Temptation purifies the beginner by reminding him of past sins, committed through a lack of vigilance, and inciting renewed contrition. Thus, temptation is a means of spiritual progress, goading the soul to forge ahead toward a higher goal. Since beginners suffer from inconstancy, resisting temptation through force of will helps them to strengthen virtue.

The Intermediate Process of Illumination

The second Exposition (2295-3306) introduces the process of Illumination, with its emphasis on grace as God labors to cleanse the soul, adorn it with virtue, and restore the <u>Imago Dei</u>. The advancing soul begins to experience God in affective meditation, a difference in prayer reflected in Nassington's choice of language, as he no longer urges the soul to yearn to see God, but now to feel and to taste his sweetness through the spiritual senses. As the soul meditates on Christ, expecially in his Passion and Death, it begins to imitate his virtue. For when the eyes of the soul are continually on Christ, the soul begins to share His dispositions, and to follow His example. As the advanced soul reflects upon Christ in His mercy, it will, for example, begin to practice mercy. As the soul advances in the Illuminative way, Christ becomes the center of thought and affection.

In introducing the unique work of the Seven Gifts of the Holy Spirit in the Second Exposition of the <u>Speculum Vitae</u>, Nassington develops the doctrine of grace that is central to the <u>Speculum Vitae</u>. The three intellectual Gifts -- Wisdom,

Understanding, and Counsel -- illumine the soul, preparing it for mystical union.[5] Wisdom, according to St. Bernard, is knowledge which relishes divine things through its twofold elements: light to enlighten the mind, and supernatural taste which acts on the will. Understanding reveals insight into the harmony between God and the soul, centering on the heart of God's life and mysteries so the soul becomes attached to spiritual truths. Counsel enables the soul to apply the light of the Holy Spirit to human acts as an adjunct to reason. Wisdom, Understanding, and Counsel have in common their power to provide the soul with experiential knowledge of divine things, not attainable through reason but through the higher light of the Holy Spirit.

The Gifts of the intellect are assisted by the four other Gifts: Fortitude, Knowledge, Piety and Fear. Fortitude imparts to the will an impulse enabling it to do virtuous acts with joy and without fear, even to endure martyrdom. Knowledge perfects faith, leading the soul to consider objects in their proper origin, to detach oneself from creatures, and to form sound judgments about sanctification. Piety begets a filial affection for God and a tender devotion toward those persons and things consecrated to Him. Fear perfects faith against the inordinate longing for pleasure, delivering the soul from the perils of this world and the next. Thus the Seven Gifts of the Holy Spirit are the divine promptings by which the <u>Imago Dei</u> is restored to the soul.

The Second Exposition, introducing the work of Wisdon, illustrates Nassington's dependency upon the mystical language of the spiritual senses:

> He tastes þe sauour what it ys,
> And feles of Gode þe swetnes
> As he þat wille and may tast wele
> þe swytnes of gude likour and fele
> Be þe mouthe, if he tast right,
> Better þan he may by þe sight (2380-2385).

The soul engages in affective meditation through the spiritual senses, which are the products of the Gifts of Wisdom and Understanding.[6] The spiritual sense of sight enables the soul to see God and divine things, the sense of hearing to listen to Him speaking in the heart. The spiritual senses also cause the soul to breathe the fragrance of perfection, to feel the touch of a spiritual embrace, or to savour the taste of divine love, implying a spiritual knowledge of God.

Wolfgang Riehle's comprehensive study of the language of the <u>Middle English Mystics</u> traces the concrete image of directly eating and tasting God, of consuming God as an image for union, as an outgrowth of the symbolism for the Eucharist, revived in the High Middle Ages.[7] Such a spiritual knowledge of God, expressed by Rolle as "savouren," or "felen," especially in the context of the Passion, takes on the meaning of reenacting, or sharing an experience, rather than the modern-day emotional connotation of feeling.[8] Nassington often uses "felen" as used by these Middle English mystics, either to express spiritual knowledge, or spiritual experience. The term describes the ultimate goal of perfection, the possession of God as felt in the soul.

Because English mysticism is rooted in the tradition of St. Bernard and St. Francis, it is primarily Christocentric. This emphasis on the incarnation of Christ as God and man, symbolizing the union between the human and divine, results in words such as "onen" and its cognates, which commonly appear in medieval descriptions of mystical union.[9] The author of The Cloud of Unknowing describes mystical union as the effort "to knythip þe ghastely knot," and Walter Hilton instructs his audience to "knythiþ þe knette of leve and devotion to Ihjsu," both adaptions of the secular love-knot metaphor used in a spiritual context. The love motif of unfulfilled love-longing, basic to people of all ages, appears in scriptural texts, especially the Song of Songs, which are the ultimate source of mystical language. Nassington's most frequent term to illustrate the union of God and the soul is "festen" although like the other English mystics, he substitutes common synonyms such as "binden," "knitten," "couplen," and "joinen."

The imagery of God as light is found in almost all religions; in the Old Testament God is described as a cleansing fire.[10] Nassington begins his exposition of the work of Wisdom in the soul with the image of a refining fire, as God draws the soul into good works and dedicated service. This total commitment to God is a second baptism, a baptism of blood, and the fruit of affective prayer. Nassington makes a comparison between the soul consecrated to God and the Eucharistic consecration:

> And when he thynkes vp and doone
> On Cryst and on hys passion,
> It ys thurgh litted in þe blode
> þat Cryst schede for hym on þe rode,
> As a sope ys of warme brede
> þat ys dibbed in wyne rede,
> So ys þe hert þat ys clene to fele
> In the blod of Cryst lyttede wele (2428-2435).

Wisdom (14,899-15,192), the highest Gift, draws the soul into mystical union:

> A gret grace þis, þis at þe last
> When þe hert in Gode ys so rotefast,
> þat þe wille and þi deuocion
> May noȝt be loused thurgh temptacon
> And so fulfylled in þi luf anely
> Of þe swetenes of God allemyghty,
> þat it ne may no solace gyte,
> Bot of Gode þar þe thoght ys sette,
> þan ys þe hert þat þis may fele
> Festend in Gode perfytely and wele (2470-79).

Through the Gift of Understanding (2502-2597), God works to cleanse and illuminate the soul, restoring the Imago Dei. Understanding clarifies the soul's perception of revealed truth, such as the meaning of the prophecies disclosed to the disciples on the way to Emmaus. When God possess the soul so completely that it sees spiritual truths, it seeks God as its only treasure. Nassington illustrates the clarity effected by Understanding through the Gospel parable of the treasure hidden in the field.

The Third Gift, Counsel (2598-2663), acquired by learning to listen to the Holy Spirit, advances the soul's progress by turning the Will toward God:

> þat na self wille, ne wyt in vs rest,
> Bot ys wille anely þat ys best,
> þat it be huswyf and lady
> Of alle þe hert with in haly,
> And gouerne it with reson and skylle,
> And do in vs what so it wille (2617-2622).

Counsel and the two intellectual gifts of Wisdom and Understanding make thought more penetrating, and love more ardent, enabling the soul to gaze affectionately on God as truth during contemplation.

Fortitude, the Fourth Gift (2664-2887), strengthens the soul, especially through the Eucharist. Fortitude takes hold of the soul, giving it domination over the lower faculties and over temptation. It permits the soul to undertake difficult tasks and to endure painful trials of body and soul. Nassington directs that the Eucharist be received with "birnand luf (2741)" and extols the efficacy of this Sacrament:

> Þis ys bred of þat blyssed couent,
> þe brede of hewyn þat he salle hent,
> þe bred of angels profytabylle,
> þe bred mast delicious and delectabylle,
> þe bred of mast sikernes,
> þe bred of lyf þat ys endeles,
> For a sekyr lyf makys þat brede.
> And keps þe saule fra gastely dede;
> þat bred may be cald right
> Fode of grete vertue and myght,
> For it many stanche wele and fylle
> Alle þe hungre of þe werld by skylle,
> And so may do no othir fode,
> Bot þat brede anely þat ys so good,
> þat bred men resaues right
> In the sacrement of þe awter dight (2699-2714).

The Fifth Gift, Knowledge (2888-3107), helps the conscience to distinguish between good and evil, to do penance, and to

seek forgiveness at the court of Mercy. Knowledge enables the
soul to see with eyes of faith, to make right use of created things,
and to see the image of God in them. Knowledge promotes contrition
by assisting the soul to see perfection in all of God's creatures,
for the follower of Christ must learn to love even his enemies:

>As a lyme lufs of þe body,
>And for beres ane othir lym kyndly
>If þe tane hurt þe tothir sare,
>þe tother wenges it never þe mare
>We er in Crist alle a body,
>As says þe bok openly (3012-3017).

Nassington illustrates the prayer of a contrite soul:

>Lord for gyf me here my dettes
>þat er my synnes þat my mede lettes,
>For why I am, as þu may se,
>Gretely endetted onence þe
>Thurgh my wyckdnes þat I haue wroght
>In word, in werk, in wille, in toght,
>And for þe good þat I have left to do,
>And þat I haue for gyttyn þar to
>þat I shuld haue done thurgh skylle,
>And myght haue done and had no wille (3074-3082).

The Sixth Gift, Piety (3108-3148), perfects the gift of religion,
heightening the necessity for spiritual exercises, increasing the
yearning to sacrifice for God, and encouraging abandonment to
the will of God. Piety strengthens the soul through the
temptations of the world, the flesh, and the devil, as Nassington
explains:

>Bot when he þat temptes, says saynt Bernard,
>Vpon our bakkes strikys herd,
>He forges vs crones of blys
>þat God graunts to þam þat er his (3137-3140).

Piety also stabilized the relationship of the soul with God in preparation for its growth into Virtue:

> Þat is a grace þat freshes þe hert wele,
> And maks it swet and piteous to fele,
> And makys it floryshe, as says þes clerkys,
> And beere fruyt inoghe of good werkys,
> And festyns his rotys in þe land (3159-3163).

The Seventh Gift, Fear (3249-3277), fosters discursive prayer as the soul proceeds on the way of perfection:

> To say a pater noster wele
> With a right vndirstandyng,
> And with deuocion and lyknge,
> Þan a thosand to say ouer thwert
> With outyn deuocion of hert (3320-3324).

Fear makes the sense of God's greatness vivid, increases sorrow for offending Him, and removes one from occasions of sin. Fear of displeasing God or being separated from Him begins to detach the soul from the pleasure that leads to evil. Nassington concludes the introduction of the Gifts in the Second Exposition by reminding his audience of the prime importance of the Petitions which name spiritual graces over those that name the temporal means of salvation.

The Gifts of Counsel and Understanding initiate illumination through the virtues of Mercy and Chastity, as given in the Third Exposition. Mercy must eradicate Avarice, and Chastity supplant Lechery. Avarice, the desire for worldly possessions, extends to all persons, like a tree with ten sprawling branches (6167-6344). Nassington's topical illustrations of these branches, discussed in Chapter Three, reveal the autobiographical nature of the

Speculum Vitae. Greed is replaced by practicing the spiritual works of mercy (7638-8265), the corporal works of mercy (8266-8825), and by alms giving (8826-9269). The spiritual works of mercy include comforting the needy, teaching by good example, chastising those who have sinned, forgiving those who have wronged, forgiving all wrongs, feeling compassion for those in tribulation, and praying for one's enemies. The seventh work, prayer, is a source of comfort and a means of growth in virtue. Nassington instructs his audience to meditate on the pains of hell, the joys of paradise, the Passion of Christ, or their individual gifts of grace. Through meditation, a soul will place its personal suffering in the perspective of Christ's redemptive suffering:

>   To thynk ay on Crystes passioun,
>   þat he tholed for mans trespas,
>   Wha so thynkes how hard it was,
>   Furst how he had many sare buffet
>   And sithen was naked with scorges bett,
>   þat ys body ran alle on blode
>   And sithen naled was on þe rode,
>   And þar on he dyed and ʒelded þe gast
>   And alle tholed he for our luf mast,
>   So hard payn had neuer man,
>   As Cryst for vse suffertt þan (8109-8119).

Next, Nassington outlines the corporal works of mercy as an additional means to practice virtue:

>   Ane ys hungre and thirsty to fede
>   With mett and drynk þat has nede,
>   Anothir ys ay when nede ware
>   To cloth þam þat er nakyd and bare,
>   þe third ys to fryst þam for Goddys sak
>   þat has gret nede of fryst to tak,
>   And of þe dett to gyf respett,

> And pam for gyf þat may noȝt qwytt,
> þe four, as men vndirstandes,
> To vnsett þat lyen in Goddys bandes,
> þe fyft ys poer men to herber
> And poer pylgryms þat walkyn fere,
> þe sext ys as in bok ys fundern
> To wesset þam þat er in preson bunden,
> þe seuent ys to bery þe dede (8268-8282).

Scripture and hagiography provide Nassington with numerous illustrations of Mercy, such as the miraculous healings of Christ, and St. Martin's gift of his cloak to the poor. He concludes the section by paraphrasing the Gospel story anticipating the last judgment, when those who were merciful will be called to everlasting Mercy, as promised in the Fifth Beatitude.

Understanding uproots Lechery, forbidden acts and thoughts which diminish the desire for perfection and the relish for prayer (9418-9779). Chastity counters Lechery, checking inordinate pleasure and filling the heart with affection for God and devotion to the duties of one's state in life (9780-13,224). Lechery of the heart is defined with four divisions:

> Lychory ys ane outrageous luf
> In fleshly lykynge, as clerkys can pruf,
> In whilk þe fende can a man lede
> Thurgh four thynges vnto þe dede,
> A thynge ys foule sight of h[is] eghe,
> Anouthir ys speche of wordes sleghe,
> þe third ys foule techyng with hand,
> þe fourth ys kyssyng next folowand,
> And sone þe lycherus dede folous pan,
> To whilk þe fend þus ledys a man (9418-9427)

Nassington's four conditions of sin explain the complex teaching about full consent of the will to an uneducated audience:

> Ane ys toght, a nothir ys delytt
> þat may fale in þe hert tyte,
> þe thyrd ys consentynge of skylle·,
> þe fourth ys ȝernyng to do þat wille (9470-9473).

The divisions of Lechery of the body are determined by one's state in life, whether single, wedded or vowed; however, Lechery in prelates and other religious men and women consecrated to Chastity is most foul and subject to God's vengeance.

Nassington gives seven practical ways to acquire the virtue of Chastity:

> Þe fyrste degre ys þis to be gyn
> Clene conscyence of herte with in,
> þe secunde degre falles to be couthe
> þat ys honest speche with mouthe,
> þe third ys kepyng of þe wyttes fyue,
> þe fourth ys herdnes of strayt lyue,
> þe fyft ys sleyng of foule company
> And þe enchesons of foly,
> þe sext ys good occupacioun
> þe seuent ys prayer of devocioun (9786-9795).

Devout prayer, a thousand-line digression (10,201-11,176), is Nassington's seventh degree of Chastity and his argument for a firm defense against Lechery. Prayer is the essential means through which the soul obtains grace, a teaching Nassington verifies in the words or writing of many authorities, including Christ, St. Bernard, St. Ambrose, Isidore, St. James, St. Augustine, St. Jerome, St. Cyprian, St. Gregory, St. Anselm, the evangelists and St. Paul. The object for the beginner is to turn the soul to the presence of God in vocal prayer; one comes before God through petition and worship, expressed by word and gesture. In contrast, mental prayer takes place within the soul, as the mind and heart are elevated to God for His glory and the growth of the soul. As the soul considers the necessity of Christ's death and Passion in atonement for sin, it becomes detached from sin, from the world and its false pleasures, resulting in contrition and a firm purpose of amendment. Because meditation initiates union with God, it prepares the soul for the restoration of the Imago Dei.

Affective meditation is conversation with God in which reasoning becomes less prominent, and which becomes more intimate, more tender, and longer, even in the midst of life's activities. As the soul meditates on the great Christian truths, such as the end of man, creation, the elevation of man to supernatural life, the fall and redemption, the attributes of God, and on the great Christian duties, including the individual obligation to expiate sin, to be faithful to one's responsibilities, and to be loyal to grace, it will advance in virtue in imitation of Christ.[11] In affective prayer, the heart is engaged to a greater extent than the mind in acts of will, expressing love of God and the desire to glorify Him. The soul easily admires, adores, thanks, pities, loves, praises, and blesses the God who loves him so greatly. In order to demonstrate his love, the soul seeks to resemble the virtues exemplified in Christ.

The prayer of the perfected soul is different from that of the beginner, although it continues to consider sin, penance, and mortification. The soul works to detach itself from created things in order to unite with Christ, to consider Him loaded down with its transgressions through the Passion and Death. Affective prayer brings one into conformity with God's will, increases the desire to give glory to God, love of silence and recollection, the desire for the Eucharist, and the spirit of sacrifice. The soul experiences a spiritual consolation in the companionship of Christ, and it lingers with pleasure, wonder and love on the mysteries of God.

Nassington guides the beginner with practical suggestions on prayer: how to avoid distraction, how to be attentive and devout. He recommends the Sabbath, principal feasts, liturgical cycle of Christ's birth, death and resurrection, and the feast of Pentecost as times of worship. He gives his audience practical rules of decorum for worship, good manners and appropriate dress for church. Prayer, Nassington concludes, is grounded on four pillars: faith, hope, devotion, and fasting with alms giving (10,221-11,176).

Even the pagan philosophers prepared themselves for contemplation by chastising the body and denying the senses, which are practices Nassington advocates for each of the seven states of Chastity:

>   Ane ys meydyns þat wille fle
>   Fleshly dedys tille þai maryd be,
>   Anothir ys anelopy
>   þat has bene fylled and leues par foly
>   þe third ys of þam þat wedde bene,
>   þe fourt state ys of wydows clene,
>   þe fyft ys of maydyns sley

>þat thynkes be chast vn tille pai dye,
>þe sext state of clerkys may be
>þat er ordaned in haly degre,
>þe seuent, as be bok makys mencioun,
>Ys of men of religioun (11,185-11,196).

Because the <u>Imago Dei</u> is clearest in the souls of virgins, Nassington envisions them in the highest place in heaven.

As the soul advances in perfection, it experiences more intense joy as well as increased difficulty. The aridity of soul experienced when God withdraws his consolation is described as a wilderness, a metaphor that was later taken from the <u>Speculum Vitae</u> and expanded in the fifteenth century <u>Desert of Religion</u>:[12]

>Religioun þat God shuld hald
>May be slyk deserte cald,
>For as deserte ys comonly sene
>In sharp sted per na delites bene,
>And ȝit fere fro man deserte ys
>perfor men calles it wyldernes,
>Right so þe state of religioun,
>þat falles to lyf of perfeccoun (12,813-12,820).

Despite the continual trials, the process of illumination restores the <u>Imago Dei</u> to the soul.

>Pis blyssed hede þat here ys
>Salle be fullfilled in þe lyf endeles,
>þer clene man of herete clere
>Thurghe trouth may se hym here,
>And dym þat sight behoues be,
>Bot þer salle þai hym appertely see
>Face to face thurghe clere sight,
>As says Saynt Paul þe apostelle bright;
>þis ys þe blyssed hede of anngels
>And to balous þat in hewyn dwelles,
>þat ay may Gode in his face se
>And a God knawe in persons thre,
>And be hald thurghe grete lykynge
>In þe meroure brightest of alle thynge (13,123-13,136).

Mystical Union as the Goal of Perfection (13,225-16,395)

The mystic experiences union with God through the Gift of Wisdom, which resides in the intellect, infusing the will with both light and love.[13] St. Bernard teaches that Wisdom contains light which illumines the mind to judge all created things in accord with their ultimate principles, and it gives a supernatural taste which acts upon the will enabling it to relish divine things. Wisdom is manifest as light which illumines and delights the eyes of the soul and as heat that warms the heart, enflames it with love, and fills it with joy. In contrast to the insight of the mind through Understanding, Wisdom is an experience undertaken by the heart and cultivated by the longing for God that incites the soul to undertake a journey of perfection. Thus, union with God in mystical prayer is the fulfillment of the spiritual exercises of purgation and the affective meditation of illumination. According to Nassington, Wisdom satisfies all the soul's yearnings:

> Þis ys þe heghest gyft and þe mast,
> Þat makes a man to fele and tast
> Þe grete swetnes and þe savour
> Of Gode allemyghty his creatour
> So þat hym thynk no thynge erdely
> Ys so swete, no so sauery,
> Þan he settes alle his lykynge
> Anley in Gode ouer alle thynge (13,231-13,238).

This highest step of perfection, according to Nassington's Third Exposition, is stifled by Gluttony, that is, by abusing the ordinate pleasures attached to eating and drinking (13,247-14,898). It is tempered by Soberness (14,899-16,275), which

keeps these pleasures in their proper order. Gluttony is overindulgence of the tongue, evidenced in eating and drinking and in
speech:

>   Glotony, as þes clerkes proves,
>   Ys a syn þat þe belly luffes,
>   þe whilk thre thynges of mas wastes
>   Mete and drynke in outrage tastes,
>   Furst it wastes þe saul with in
>   For it ys a foul dedely syn,
>   It wastes the body and for duse
>   Thurgh unkynd outrage use
>   It wastes hys goodes thurgh outrage
>   Of oþer grete dispens and costage (13,283-13,292).

St. Gregory is named as Nassington's source for the seven branches
of Gluttony (13,403-13,779):

>   Outhir to ete or drynk over tymely,
>   Or ouer outragely thurghe wille,
>   Or ouer hastely agayn skille,
>   Or ouer daynte nously thurgh talent,
>   Or ouer besily about mete to tent (13,398-13,402)

Colorful exempla similar to those in the Prick of Conscience,
including a dialogue between the belly and the purse, illustrate
Nassington's commentary on the seven branches. His narrative
on the tavern as the devil's chapel recounts the miracles worked
there, when a person enters with his senses but leaves without
his "Wyte, and mynde, and undirstandynge (13,821)," which
three faculties are essential to contemplation.

Overindulgence in speech, the second aspect of Gluttony, is
also divided into ten categories:

>   Idille speche, and wayne vauntunge,
>   Losengery, and bakbytynge,
>   Leynge, forswerynge thurgh athe,
>   Stryfynge, and gruchynge bathe,

> Frawardnes, and sclaundir neuen
> To Gode and his halous of hewyn (13,885-13,890).

While these ten branches are sins of an idle tongue, they stem from a wicked heart. The last, slander, renews the suffering of the Passion and can never be forgiven, since it is a sin against the Holy Spirit:

> Þat is when men sweres vilany,
> Or þer be Gode, or be his myght,
> Or be his halous in newyn bright,
> Or be his saul, or be his herte,
> Or þe payn þat sare gune smerte,
> Or be his fleche, or be his blode,
> Or be his dede þat he tholed on rode,
> Be his fete, or handes twa,
> Be his nales [on] fynger and ta.
> Or be his body, or his banes,
> Or alle his lymes neuened at anes (14,420-14,430).

Soberness, however, uproots Gluttony for it balances reason and Understanding, frees the soul from its slavery to the body, and bridles the senses, "Þe gates of the castelle (15,197)," guarding the body's holiness. Nassington suggests three ways to practice Soberness:

> Ane is kynd to lede with skille,
> Anoþer ys haly wyrte to fullefylle,
> þe third ys ilk a creature right
> þat Gode has made thurgh myght (15,233-15,236).

Practicing temperance keeps the soul under the rule of reason, draws it from the attraction of the world, and prepares it for union, experienced through the spiritual senses:

> Þis ys þe hight of perfeccion
> And þe ende of contemplacion,
> Þe haly gyft of undirstandynge
> Of whilk I have said befor some thynge,
> Mas þe hert to knawe Gode right
> And gastely thynges thurgh gastely sight,

> Bot þe gyft of wysdome þat ys maste
> Mas it to knawe fele and tast,
> For wysdome ys no noþer thynge
> Bot a swete savory knawynge,
> þat ys to say þat sauours wele
> þat þe hert with delytt may fele (14,917-14,928).

In the remainder of the Speculum Vitae, Nassington describes how the purified soul experiences union with God. Discursive prayer and affective meditation are simplified in union, for the soul lingers lovingly on thoughts of God.[14] In a general way, contemplation means looking with admiration on an object, so supernatural contemplation means an affectionate gaze on God or divine things. It excludes the long reasonings of discursive prayer and the multiplicity of acts which characterize affective prayer. The soul's activity may be alternated with special graces in which God takes hold of the soul, infusing it with light and affection. Whether active or passive, the prayer of mystical union is one of simplicity.

In the prayer of union, the soul fastens its affectionate gaze on God, remains in His presence, yields to His action, and, through a simple unreasoned faith, loves Him. Reasoning is replaced by a gentle contemplation that keeps the soul at peace, attentive and receptive to communications of the Holy Spirit. The contemplative soul does little and receives much; its labor is sweet and fruitful. Because the soul approaches the source of all light and grace, it profits from an increased share in virtue.

The beginner in prayer reflects at length on fundamental religious truths before the heart brings forth sentiments of gratitude, love, contrition, and amendment. When these convictions become habitual, pious affections easily spring forth. As the soul advances in prayer, another simplification takes place: reflection is replaced by an intuitive intellectual gaze. Having frequently meditated on spiritual truths, it grasps them at a glance without lengthy analyses. For example, the concept of Father, which required repetition of the Pater Noster, appears so fruitful that the advanced soul lingers with it lovingly to relish the elements. Thus, the style of each mystic is revealed in his choice of language. Richard Rolle sensed God as heat, sweetness, and song. Nassington fastens his gaze on the divine, relishing rest, joy, and peace:

>Þis salle be pees maste profitabille,
>þees mast honorabille and delitabille,
>þees mast sekir and stedfast,
>þees mast perfyte þat ay salle last,
>þees þat alle thynges salle passe (16,246-16,250).

The affections, too, are simplified. For the beginner, they are varied and follow one another in quick succession, such as sentiments of love, gratitude, joy, compassion, sorrow for sin, desire for amendment, and supplication. As the soul advances in prayer without expressing itself in words, one affection absorbs the soul for prolonged periods. The soul ceases to multiply dispositions, as one or more affection becomes dominant, such as devotion for Christ in His Passion, which stirs the heart with sentiments of love and sacrifice.

Nassington describes mystical union as the special grace, a result of Christ's Redemption, denied the pagan philosophers. Because they were given reason and understanding they had knowledge of God through the Book of Nature, comprehending His beauty, bounty, and divine might. But it is the grace of Wisdom alone that draws the soul deep into mystical union (13,225-13,246; 14,899-15,541).

> Þare he hym fedes wele and greses
> Þer he hym sustans and eses,
> Þer he hym delites and hym kepis
> And Þar he ligges, ristes and slepis,
> Þer forgyttes he alle worldly thynges
> His trauails and his ʒernynges,
> Þat er fleshly and also erthly
> And alle hym self enence his body,
> So Þat he thynkes on na thynge elles
> Bot on thynges of whilk his luf dwelles,
> Þat is anely of Gode of hewyn
> Þat is his mast comfurth to neuyn (14,969-14,980).

God's possession of the soul in mystical union causes a profound state of recollection. The soul contemplates the majesty of God within, delights in the happiness of its possession, finds unspeakable rest, fulfills all its earthly longing. Nassington paraphrases Augustine's expression of the soul's desire to possess and to be possessed by God:

> Saynt Austayn says Lord my hert
> May noʒt be in pees in whert
> Tille at it may rest in Þe
> Þer pees and rest salle euer be (15,346-15,349).

Because God is not experienced through reason, but by intuition, the soul struggles with the impossibility of describing mystical union. One reason is that the mind is plunged into

God's infiniteness, which is only vaguely comprehended. Also the experience of God is so intense, the mystic lacks language to describe it. The finite mind can never perceive the divine essence; it can only know what God is not, as described in the prominent <u>Cloud of Unknowing</u>. In mystical union, the soul is impressed with transcendent, ardent love for Him Whose goodness cannot be expressed but Who fills the soul. For most mystics, union produces a profound sense of joy. Mystical union is achieved through grace, yet paradoxically only known through experience.

Nassington portrays the stairway to mystical union as the ladder, the image used by the Old Testament Jacob which reappears in Dante's Canto XXI of <u>Paradisio</u>, the <u>Ladder of Four Rungs</u> and Walter Hilton's <u>Scale of Perfection</u>. Angels lead the soul from virtue to virtue, from earth to heaven:

>   Vntille þai Gode appertly se
>   Thurgh luf in perfite charite,
>   When þai clymbe so he
>   Vntille þe heghest degre of þe ste (14,999-15,022).

The highest experience of mystical union fills the heart with generosity to instruct others in the way of perfection:

>   Fra þat high contemplacion
>   Behouves oft sith [to] come don,
>   Fra þat swetnes and þe rest
>   And þat delyte þat þam thynk best,
>   Whilk þai fele of þe pappes swete
>   Of comfurth when þai with þam mete,
>   þat Gode to þam lufly biddes
>   Then gyffes at sonk and fedes,
>   In whilk a lyf contemplatyfe
>   Vnto werkys of actif lyfe (15,031-15,040).

Historically, contemplation does not hamper but directs and enlightens action. Contemplation in action is the direct consequence of the unitive life, impelling the mystic to return and serve the world, following the example of Christ. Saints such as John Chrysostom, Ambrose, Augustine, Anselm, Thomas Aquinas, Teresa of Avila, and Catherine of Siena are exemplars of contemplation-in-action.

The research of Ray Petry and Richard Kieckhefer demonstrates the secular and ecclesial service of figures such as Raymund Lull, Meister Eckhardt, John Tauler, Richard Rolle, the <u>Cloud</u> author, John Ruysbroeck, and Nicholas of Cusa.[15] The Middle English mystics also represent the concept of contemplation-in-action through their lives and writings. Walter Hilton describes the fusion of action and contemplation in his treatise, <u>On the Mixed Life</u>. Souls gifted with the grace of contemplation are impelled to prophetic action, to defeat ignorance, injustice, corruption, and forces opposing the Body of the Church. The mixture of action and contemplation, symbolized by the union of Martha and Mary, is popular in the writings of the female continental mystics, where it is often discussed as spiritual fecundity.[16]

Such mystical union, binding God and the soul, inflaming the soul to action, is a transitory experience. Nassington explains that it:

> Is nathynge bot a lyttle tast
> thurgh whilk men feles mast
> Of God þat ys so swet and soft (15,073-15,075).

He incorporates a number of traditional images to describe the mystical vision, such as the Psalmist David's image of God as a well of everlasting life:

> In paradyce and þat salle be
> A blysfulle flode of grete plente,
> Of joy, and delyte, and pees,
> And of rest þat neuer salle sese,
> So grete þat alle þat drynkes of þis
> Salle be drunkyn of joy of blis,
> þis þe blys and þe blissed hede
> þat perfyte men salle haue to mede
> In þis werld þat is to come
> Thurgh þe gyft of high wysdome (15,119-15,128).

Later he presents the vision as a heavenly city, like the traditional metaphor of Augustine used by the <u>Pearl</u> poet. The celestial city stands alone on a rock, that is the Lord, and on that rock stands a castle from which flows a well of love:

> Þis welle is so clere and bright
> þat þe herte may se be gastely sight,
> In it þat is so clere of coloure
> And knawe hymself and his creature,
> As a man seys thurgh þe ayre
> Hym selfe in a welle clere and fayr,
> On þis welle þe hert it restes
> þat aftir þe luf of Gode threstes (15,366-15,373).

Nassington elaborates upon the metaphor, envisioning God as the clear well in which the pure soul finds its perfect image, and consequently where it wishes to rest for all eternity. Wisdom transforms the soul with the incomprehensible joy promised by the Seventh Beatitude:

> Þai er be right God sonnes cald
> For pees þai kepe wille and hald,
> For þai bere right lykenes
> Of the fadir þat Gode ys,
> And lord of pees and of lufe (16,179,-16,183).

> Whilk is þe kyngdome of hewyn,
> Per þai salle bein sekyr pees
> And perfyte joy þat neuer salle ses,
> þer þair willynges and þer ȝernynges
> Salle be fulfilled in alle thynges (16-238-16,242).

Bereft of additional words to express the ineffable vision of God, Nassington paraphrases St. Paul:

> Alle wordes of man it passes þan,
> Na hert of man thynk it may,
> Ne eer here, ne tong say,
> Ne egh se thurgh sight,
> War it neuer so clere so bright,
> What joy it is þat neuer endes
> þe pees þat Gode has hight his frendes (16,255-16,261).

Peace, defined by Augustine as the tranquility of order, is the promise of the Eighth Beatitude:

> Blissed be þai þus says he
> þat er pesabille as þai shuld be,
> þai salle be cald thurgh right
> Goddes childer þat er fulle of myght (16,272-16,275).

Thus, Nassington's lyrical description of mystical union concludes the <u>Speculum Vitae</u>. The remaining lines review the structure, stress the action of the Gifts of the Holy Spirit, call attention to the metaphor of the <u>speculum</u>, and remind the audience that the book is a mirror of life. The final lines of Nassington's treatise on the <u>via mystica</u> include prayers for his Latin source, John Waldeby, for himself, and for his audience:

> Graunte you grace here so to lyf,
> þat ȝe may come when ȝe hyns wend
> To þe blys with outyn ende,
> To whilk blys he us brynge
> þat on þe cross for us wald hynge (16,391-16,396).

Whereas the Ancrene Wisse, the first Middle English text treating contemplation, was originally intended as a rule of life for three recluses, the Speculum Vitae's audience included a broad range of educated laity and religious men and women. While it provided a guide for these devout individuals in their personal quest for God, it is unique in that it also met the demands of the reform movement through its compiled doctrine. The Speculum Vitae, measured by the evidence of its circulation in fourteenth-century manuscripts, was surpassed in popularity only by one other religious work, the Prick of Conscience.[17] The comprehensiveness of Nassington's Speculum Vitae proves him to be a speculum of late medieval England: orthodox in his doctrine, dedicated to reform, enriched by his heritage of faith, and searching for intimate union with God through the via mystica.

NOTES

[1] Eric Colledge, The Medieval Mystics of England (London: John Murray) 1962, p. 21.

[2] Colledge, pp. 101-102, recommends further studies: Pierre Courcelle, "Tradition neo-platonicienne et traditions chrétiennes de la 'region de dissemblance'," Archives d'histoire doctrinale et litteraire du Moyen Age, 24 (1957), p. 5-33.

[3] Bede's use of the image was borrowed by St. Bernard who transmitted it to Tauler and Ruysbroek. See L. Reypens, S. J., "De 'Gulden Penning' bij Tauler en Ruusbroec," Ons Geestelijk Erf 24 (1950), p. 70-79, in Colledge, p. 102.

[4] Walter Hilton, The Scale of/or Ladder of Perfection, ed., J. B. Dalgairnes (New York: Art and Book Company, 1901).

[5] A. Tanqueray, The Spiritual Life; A Treatise on Ascetical and Mystical Theology, trans., Herman Branderis (Tournai: Deslee and Co., 1930), pp. 609-31. My initial study of ascetical theology was from Tanqueray from whom I have drawn definitions and explanations for this chapter.

[6] Tanqueray, p. 635.

[7] Wolfgang Riehle, The Middle English Mystics, trans., Bernard Standring (London: Routledge and Kegan Paul, 1981), p. 107.

[8] Riehle, pp. 110-13.

[9] Riehle, pp. 89-91, provides the survey of texts mentioned in this paragraph.

[10] Riehle, p. 80.

[11] Tanqueray, pp. 461-69, discusses affective prayer more fully.

[12] Walter Hübner, "The desert of religion," Archiv für das Studium neueren Sprachen und Literaturen, 126 (1911), p. 58-74.

[13] Tanqueray, p. 629.

[14] Tanqueray, pp. 649-61, discusses mystical union.

[15] Ray C. Petry, "Social Responsibility and the Late Medieval Mystics," Church History, 21 (1952), p. 3-9; and Richard Kieckhefer, "Mysticism and Social Consciousness in the Fourteenth Century," Revue de L'Universite d'Ottawa/University of Ottawa Quarterly, 48 (1978), 179-86. See also Louis B. Pascoe, "Jean Gerson: Mysticism, Conciliarism, and Reform," Annuarium Historiae Conciliorum, 6:2 (1974), p. 135-53; Walter H. Beale, "Walter Hilton and the Concept of "Medled Lyf," ABR 26, p. 381-94; J. P. H. Clark, "Action and Contemplation in Walter Hilton," Downside Review, 97 (1979), p. 258-74; Harvey D. Egan, "Mystical Crosscurrents," Communio (7), p. 4-23.

[16] Valerie Lagorio, "Social Responsibility and the Medieval Women Mystics on the Continent," Analecta Cartusiana, (1982).

[17] Carleton Brown, A Register of Middle English Religious and Didactic Verse, Vol. 2 (Oxford: University Press, 1920), ix.

CHAPTER V

MINOR WORKS ATTRIBUTED TO NASSINGTON

In addition to the manuscript evidence attributing the Speculum Vitae to Nassington, incipits in MSS. Lincoln Cathedral 91 (Thornton) and B. L. Additional 33995 attribute the Tractatus de Trinitate et Unitate to Nassington.[1] In 1886 Carl Horstmann credited this poem to Nassington on the basis of the incipit in the Thornton manuscript, noting that the same text and incipit were included in George Perry's Religious Pieces in Prose and Verse Edited From Robert Thornton's MS. He also ascribed to Nassington the three minor poems and the Northern Homily collection from MS. B. L. Cotton Tiberius E. VII:

> Now the same Ms. contains, after the 'Mirror' fol. 1-81, 3 more poems: The Lamentation of St. Mary on the Passion (after St. Bernhard): a versification of the tract titled Spiritus Guidonis (from a prose text still extant in Ms. Vernon); then follows a set of homilies and legends in verse, which is a revised and greatly augmented edition of the Evangelia dominicalia in northern verse (cf. Alteng. Leg. N.F.) I have no doubt that the 3 poems mentioned - all translations - have the same author as the 'Mirror of Life,' viz. William of Nassyngton, and to him I also ascribe the additional parts in the homilies and legends of the same MS.[2]

I hold that the two incipits provide substantial manuscript evidence to include the Tractatus de Trinitate et Unitate in Nassington's canon, but I disagree with Horstmann's attribution of the minor works in the Cotton Tiberius manuscript to Nassington on the basis of contiguity only.

The Thornton manuscript is dated within the first half of the fifteenth century, and contains metrical romances, such as a part of <u>Morte Arthure</u> and <u>Octovian</u>, which is mentioned in the <u>Speculum Vitae</u>, and a variety of religious and devotional works, including Bonaventure's <u>Privite of the Passioune Ihesu Christi</u>, the <u>Speculum</u> of St. Edmund Rich, a sermon of John Gaytrick, Chapter II of Walter Hilton's <u>Scale of Perfection</u>, and an excerpt from the <u>Prick of Conscience</u>. The authors of all the works are carefully identified in the Thornton manuscript, with Nassington's <u>Trinitate</u> appearing between Bonaventure's <u>Passion</u> and four poems by Rolle.

MS. B. L. Additional 33995, dated late fourteenth century, contains four religious pieces: the <u>Speculum Vitae</u>, a poem on Hell, Purgatory, Heaven and the misery of human life, the <u>Prick of Conscience</u>, and a fragment of the <u>Trinitate</u>, called by the alternate title, <u>Bande of Lovynge</u>. This copy of the <u>Trinitate</u> includes the incipit to Nassington, whereas the copy of the <u>Speculum Vitae</u> does not include the colophon to Nassington. The scribe of MS. B. L. Additional 33995 concludes his copy of the <u>Speculum Vitae</u> with this passage:

 þat yhe pray for hym bathe alde and yhung
 þat turned þis boke to Inglisshe tung
 Whare so he be and in what stede
 Whethir he lif or he be dede.[3]

The scribe seemed to know nothing about William of Nassington as the author of the <u>Speculum Vitae</u>, and apparently copied the texts exactly as he found them in his sources. Thus, a reliable scribe appears to have copied the incipit and text of the <u>Tractatus de Trinitate et Unitate</u> in MS. B. L. 33995. Based on the evidence of the incipit, both Wells' <u>Manual</u> and Brown and Robbins' <u>Index</u> attribute the <u>Tractatus de Trinitate et Unitate</u> to Nassington.[4]

The <u>Tractatus</u> poem is a prayerful meditation, consisting of 216 short couplets, praising the Father as he is revealed in Creation, the Son in the Incarnation and Redemption, and the Spirit through the grace which leads to the joy of everlasting life. As in the <u>Speculum Vitae</u>, Nassington follows Augustine and praises the attributes of the Three Persons of the Trinity:

> A, Lorde god of myghtis maste,
> Fadere and Sone and Haly Gaste;
> Fadere for þou erte almyghtty,
> Sone for thow ert all-wyll
> That gude is, and na thynge yll;
> A gode and ane lorde yn ane-hede,
> Thus was thow aye and evere sall be,
> The yn ane, ande ane yn thre (1-10).[5]

Riehle calls attention to the Germanic form, "threhed," in the above passage, a word he has found only in the <u>Tractatus</u> of the English mystical writings.[6] Because there is no English term to express the unity of the three in one, other English texts, including the <u>Speculum Vitae</u>, use "trinite." Following his pattern in the devotional sections of the <u>Speculum Vitae</u>, Nassington interrupts a doctrinal exposition with an outpouring of personal gratitude that envelopes his audience:

>   Lovede and blyssede ay mote þou be;
>   And with all my herte I thanke the
>   Of all þat þou has done and wroughte,
>   Fra þe firste tyme þat þou began oghte,
>   For me and for all man-kynde;
>   Whare-fore us aghte ay have þe in mynde
>   And love the; for þou has done to mane
>   Als I here thurgh þi grace reherse cane (25-33).

Following this brief introductory commentary of the Three Persons of the Trinity, Nassington retells the story of Creation (33-129), for its plentitude reveals God's generosity:

>   For Ensaumple til us, to knawe & se
>   How we sulde liffe here in like a degre (57-58).

The second section in the <u>Tractatus</u>, the major part of the poem, gives events in the life of Christ (130-374), including pictorial details about the Passion, like those found in many medieval affective texts. Nassington refers to Mary's annunciation, Christ's nativity, His circumcision, baptism, temptation in the desert, way of the cross, death, deposition, burial, resurrection, appearance to the disciples and ascension. After Nassington's visual account of the Passion, using the method of affective meditation, he provides a prayer to help his audience identify with the suffering of Jesus, and to respond with contrition:

>   Lorde, for þire bitter paynes & fell,
>   With othire, ma þan I kane tel,
>   That þou swa mekill suffire walde
>   For me synfull, þi traytoure baulde,
>   I thanke þe here Inwardly
>   With all my herte and my body,
>   A, Ihesu Crist, Lorde full of myghte,
>   Whene I thynke outhire day or nyghte
>   Of swa mekill kyndned of þe,

> And of þe paynes þat þou tholide for me,
> And of myne unkyndnesse many-fawlde,
> & how I wrethe þe ay hafe bene bawlde,
> Of myne hard herte þan es gret wondire
> þat it for sorowe bristez noghte Insundyre (281-294).

In the final section of Tractatus, Nassington recounts the descent of the Holy Spirit on Pentecost (374-379), the Last Judgment, and urges his audience to ask for the mercy of God and life everlasting (380-432). With this brief scriptural account of the appearance of the Holy Spirit as comforter, Nassington concludes his exposition on the separate works of the Trinitarian God. The doctrine that the Holy Spirit is the essential grace for salvation and perfection is stated in a single line of the Tractatus poem:

> The lighte of grace þat gastely gifte es (49).

The Trinitarian structure of the Tractatus de Trinitate et Unitate corresponds to that of the Speculum Vitae. It follows the method of affective prayer, as the poet vividly recalls scenes from scripture, in this case predominantly from the life of Christ, which inspires sentiments of love and devotion.

The Tractatus is a spiritual odyssey, like the Speculum Vitae, in which Nassington interpolates his prayerful responses, and urges his audience to reflect with him on the mysteries of creation and salvation. Both the Speculum Vitae and the Tractatus end with a similar lyrical call for the reader to pursue the everlasting joy that is the goal of human life. Thus, not only the manuscripts give external evidence of Nassington's authorship on the Tractatus but the text reveals Nassington's use of affective language, and the autobiographical expressions of prayer that are the fruit of mystical union. Nassington presents orthodox doctrine, never indifferently, but with affection that enfolds his audience. His prayer is contemplation-in-action, and his poetry is a call to seek the way of perfection.

Horstmann identifies the Tractatus de Trinitate et Unitate as "mainly a reproduction of St. Edmund's Speculum," and includes a prose version from the Thornton manuscript as evidence.[7] A comparison of these works shows that while they have a thematic affinity also found in similar devotional works, Nassington's 432 lines are not taken from St. Edmund's twenty-seven chapters. Edmund's Speculum, as a guide to perfection, teaches that knowledge of God comes through contemplation of the Book of Scripture and the Book of Nature. In his final chapters on contemplation, Edmund associates the hours of the Divine Office with the events in the life of Christ. Nassington has no such reference to the canonical hours in the Tractatus. Since both of these works employ methods of affective meditation to portray the life of Christ, details in some of their passages are similar. Like St Edmund's Speculum, Nassington's Tractatus portrays creation as a speculum of God's goodness. However, even a cursory comparison of these two works indicates that Horstmann's claim, that St. Edmund's Speculum is the source of Nassington's Tractatus et Trinite et Unitate, is incorrect.

The Cotton Tiberius Manuscript

Whereas there is manuscript evidence for Nassington's authorship of the Speculum Vitae and the Tractatus de Trinitate et Unitate, the three other minor poems have been attributed to him on the basis of their contiguity in MS. B. L. Cotton Tiberius E. VII. H. L. D. Ward's Catalogue of Romances lists the contents of the Cotton Tiberius manuscript: The Speculum Vitae by William of Nassington, St. Marys Lamentation to St. Bernard on the Passion of Christ, Form of Living in verse, Spiritus Guydonis, and homilies for the liturgical year, similar to those in B. L. Harley 4196.[8] In 1886 Carl Horstmann concluded that these homilies, which are the expanded Northern Homily Collection, and the Northern Passion were by the same author.[9] Thus, by implication Horstmann also identified the Northern Passion as Nassington's.

In 1916 Francis Foster challenged both of these hypotheses on two counts.[10] Foster argued that Horstmann's evidence of parallel passages was confined to the last two hundred lines, and that the dialect in the poems was different. Secondly, he challenged Horstmann's manuscript evidence, which depended upon an erroneous dating of Cotton Tiberius E. VII, and pointed to the consistent use of the Northern Middle English a in the Speculum Vitae, whereas in St. Marys Lamentation to St. Bernard and the Northern Passion, the a and o are mixed. In dismissing the expanded Northern Passion as Nassington's, Foster implied also that the three minor poems in Cotton Tiberius were not Nassington's. Nonetheless, Wells' Manual followed Horstmann in assigning the Form of Living in verse to Nassington, together with the three works contiguous to the Speculum Vitae in MS. B. L. Cotton Tiberius E. VII.[11]

In 1972 Saara Nevanlinna, referring to the incipit establishing Nassington as author of the Tractatus de Trinitate et Unitate, found similarities to the expanded Northern Homily Cycle that suggested a single author:

> Nassyngton's tract De Trinitate could equally well be a short summary of Christ's life and passion as presented in ENHC [Enlarged Northern Homily Cycle]. The style of a great many of the homilies in ENHC resembles that of De Trinitate, with an apparently easy flow of language, but with a rather stilted rhythm and too many extra unstressed syllables crammed into scansion.[12]

However, Nevanlinna's conclusions remained inconclusive because she found similar lines in the Prick of Conscience, the Speculum Vitae, St. Marys Lamentation and the Spiritus Guydonis. Furthermore, she was unable to determine whether the textual similarities in the minor works of MS. B. L. Cotton Tiberius E. VII might be traced to a heterogeneous origin or to the scribe who put the finishing touches on the entire manuscript collection:

> He may have been a scribe in some Yorkshire scriptorium who had copied several MSS and was familiar with contemporary metrical poetry, expecially with the alliterative romances of the north-west. He must have taken an active interest in what he was writing, as scribes are often known to have done. He probably found

pleasure in adding lines here and there, and altering rhymes or words that did not appeal to him. It is not impossible that he versified a few texts himself, such as some Ferial Gospels based directly on the Bible. He must have improved the readings of many texts previously revised or versified by others, by smoothing down the roughness of the verse by small, scarcely noticeable changes. This person seems to have some epic talent. His language, reminiscent of the alliterative romances of the time, is rhythmical and easy-flowing, bearing some resemblance to Lawrence Minot's verse. Though a northerner himself, he sanctioned a number of Midland features in the rhymes of his predecessors, having come across similar ones in other texts previously copied by him.[13]

In 1978 Venetia Nelson drew similar conclusions about the individuality and interference of the Cotton Tiberius scribe:

It is the work of a scribe of independent mind and sometimes indifferent art, who deliberately and at frequent intervals throughout the poem took liberties of the kind, for example, that we find in the interpolations made in L1. 1. 8 and Harley 2260; and who also occasionally made errors of the kind found in the Vernon and Simeon MSS. The Tiberius scribe consciously altered his copy to suit himself, most often by paraphrasing, expanding or contracting lines, but also by omitting couplets he considered unnecessary (much in the manner of the scribe of Harley 435) and adding new couplets that seem to the reader to add little more to the poem than those he omitted. But in particular, it is the arbitrary and deliberate nature of the alteration that stands out. Alterations are made for their own sake; something is said in another way, a couplet is rearranged with a different rhyme, and usually no improvement is made, and often no damage is done, to the text.[14]

The unreliability of the text of the MS. B. L. Cotton Tiberius E. VII, emphasized by these recent editors, is crucial in determining Nassington's canon, for it is the only manuscript that contains all the works of questionable authorship: <u>St. Marys Lamentation to St. Bernard</u>, <u>Form of Living</u> in verse, and <u>Spiritus Guydonis</u>.

The linguistic features of these three poems, therefore, are not reliable criteria for determining authorship. Instead the poems must be examined for positive marks of Nassington: his scholarship, orthodoxy, mysticism, affective language and poetic style. The absence of these characteristics would suggest a poet other than Nassington.

St. Marys Lamentation to St. Bernard

St. Marys Lamentation to St. Bernard on the Passion of Christ is a dialogue between the Virgin Mary and St. Bernard recounting the Passion, Crucifixion and Death of Christ, in 712 stanzas. Horstmann attributes the work to Nassington and names in Latin sermon as its source, Meditatio beati Bernardi super passionem domini nostri Jesu Christi.[15] Brown and Robbins identified other copies in MSS. Vernon, Rawlinson Poetry 175, Cambridge University Library Dd 1, Trinity College Oxford 57, and Laud 463, but did not assign the poem to Nassington.[16] In 1887 K. Konrath contested Horstmann's attribution of St. Marys Lamentation to Nassington,[17] and in 1902 W. Frolich rejected Nassington, along with Rolle, because of certain rhymes containing o for Old English a.[18] Once again, Horstmann is the only proponent of Nassington's authorship, and the question remains inconclusive.

St. Marys Lamentation participates in the Planctus Mariae tradition drawn from St. Bernard's devotion to Mary, especially as seen in the Stabat Mater, the **sorrowing mother of the Crucified Christ**. Its rhetorical method of colloquy is typical of the

Planctus poems, portraying pathos in the discourse between Mary and Christ on the Cross. In St. Marys Lamentation, St. Bernard asks Mary a series of questions about the Crucifixion. In her reply she recalls the presentation of Christ in the Temple, the prophecy of Simeon, the flight into Egypt, the agony in the garden of Gethsemane, the weeping women of the Via Dolorosa, and many other vivid details of the Passion common to medieval affective writing. As Christ gives up His spirit to His Father, His last words are paraphrased:

>þir wordes er als man may se
>in ynglis tung to understand:
>"fadere, whi forsoke þou me,
>þus to be bun in bitter band?
>heder I come thurgh rede of þe:
>mi saul I send into þi hand.
>For man þus am I pined on tre:
>now es fulfilled as þou cummand" (409-416).[19]

This poem represents the extremely popular planctus tradition which emphasizes Mary's role in the Passion. Nassington does not mention Mary during his account of the Passion, although he told of her central place in the doctrine of the Annunciation and the Incarnation. Furthermore, its method of colloquy is uncharacteristic of Nassington's expository style. The autobiographical and lyrical elements that permeate the Speculum Vitae and the Tractatus do not appear in St. Marys Lament. Because Nassington's work is primarily doctrinal and mystical, not devotional, and because there is no manuscript evidence for Horstman's attribution to Nassington, the authorship of St. Marys Lamentation remains disputed.

The Form of Living

The _Form of Living_ consists of 431 octosyllabic couplets paraphrasing Chapter I-VI of Richard Rolle's _Form of Living_, a book of instruction in the spiritual life dedicated to Margaret Kirkeby, a recluse of Hampole. By its contiguity to the _Speculum Vitae_ in MS. Cotton Tiberius E. VII, it was assigned to Nassington by Horstmann, and later Ward and Waller followed Horstmann's attribution.[20] In 1974, N. F. Blake assigned the verse _Form_ to Nassington in his comparative study, "The Form of Living in Prose and Poetry."[21]

The verse _Form of Living_, like its prose counterpart, tells of three wretched conditions of mortal sin: the loss of spiritual strength, the use of fleshly sin, and the exchange of lasting goods for temporalities (1-32). Both the verse and the prose versions describe four ways the devil works among the good - deceiving them through error, vainglory, and lust, and beguiling them to do unreasonable fasting and penance (33-194). Next, both works describe three ways that the devil gains power (195-214). At this point of Chapter II in Rolle's _Form of Living_ the tribulations and joys of the solitary life are treated. In the poetic _Form_, no mention is made of the solitary life; instead the poet includes a discussion of how the devil deceives through dreams.

The next section of the verse _Form of Living_, which is badly fragmented in the Cotton Tiberius manuscript, follows the steps

to overcome sin from Chapter III of the prose text (324-395).
The verse *Form* omits a description of the holy life in terms of
the vows, but both contain four thoughts nececcary for perfection:
shortness of life, uncertainty of the end, final judgment, and the
joy of life everlasting (415-488). Following Chapter V of Rolle's
Form, the verse *Form* tells of the upward climb for those who seek
perfection (489-510), although Rolle's phrase directing the soul
to "Luf þi spouse Jhesu Criste," is omitted. Then the poetic *Form*
follows the prose Chapter VI, naming four things necessary to
know in order to follow God: what defiles a man, what makes him
clean, what keeps him clean, and what draws his will to God (511-
526). Both works contain a long section on the sins of the heart,
the mouth, sins of deed, and sins of omission (527-710).

The prose *Form* concludes in accord with Rolle's Chapter VI,
enumerating three things necessary to cleanse the soul of filth:
sorrow of heart, penance, and satisfaction (713-742), and three
ways in which to keep the heart clean (743-826). In both works
this long section describes three ways to conform the will to
God: following the example of holy men, trusting in the goodness
of the Lord, and enjoying the everlasting joy of heaven (827-862).
Rolle's discussion of the way to perfection ends here, for he
announces that the next part of his work will be on the contemplative life. In contrast, the verse *Form* adds a final note
paraphrasing St. Paul on the inexplicable joy of heaven:

> þat es gretter & more plente
> þan eres may here or eghen se
> or hertes think or tonges tell—
> wele es þam þat þare may dwell;
> and þat has gos al hallely hight.
> Vnto al þa þat lufes him right
> and honors him in stede and stall.
> Vnto þat blis he bring us all. A.M.E.N. (855-962).[22]

A comparison of the verse and prose Form of Living reveals that they are similar in content, as both works urge the audience to turn from temporal goods to begin a life of perfection. N.F. Blake correctly points out that Rolle's passages directed to the solitary life, such as the one mentioned in Chapter Two, are either omitted entirely or adapted to a more general audience in the verse Form.[23] The verse Form of Living also omits the affective language and devotion that characterized Nassington's mystical writing. In Nassington's other poems he urges his audience to join in praise with him, an imperative "mot" that does not appear in the verse Form. In the Speculum Vitae and the Tractatus the affective insight of Nassington's prayer is revealed, such as his joyful proclamations on the goodness of God. This autobiographical voice is not heard in the verse Form. For example, the poet of the verse Form describes the joy of heaven according to the authority of other clerks:

> þe ferth thing folowand es þis;
> forto think what joy and blis
> þat þaire hertes er to raviste
> þat lendes in þe luf of Criste
> lastandly ai whils þai lif,
> and al þaire hertes unto him gif;
> for þai sal be, als clerkes ken,
> breþer with angels and haly men,
> in hevyn whate þai sall plainly se
> gode in his grete maieste (459-68).

In the Speculum Vitae and the Trinitate, Nassington grounds his dogma on authority, but speaks from the fruit of his prayer about the vision of heaven.

Nassington's works show a primary emphasis on spiritual, not temporal things, on the way of perfection as the goal to mystical union. It seems unlikely that, having authored a mystical text of his own, he would take the writing of another mystic, and completely discard the section on contemplation, which is central to his own thought. The verse Form does not contain the autobiographical descriptions of mystical prayer, the lyrical affective language of joy and praise, or the urgent plea for the audience to reform their lives - all of which characterize Nassington's main work. For these reasons, I agree with Hope Emily Allen, who in 1927 suggested that the verse Form of Living should not be attributed to Nassington.[24]

Spiritus Guydonis

The Spiritus Guydonis, or Gast of Gy, a dream-vision of purgatory, is a 2125-line version of a popular prose text contained in MS. Vernon and printed by Horstmann.[25] In 1898 Gustav Schleich edited a similar text in MS. Rawlinson, together with a Latin source called De Spiritus Guidonis. Schleich contended that the poem was written by a compatriot of Richard Rolle. However, in 1972 Nevanlinna suggested that perhaps the Spiritus Guydonis was versified by Nassington,[26] thereby agreeing with Horstmann, that the 91 lines not in the Rawlinson text were the additions of the Cotton Tiberius scribe. In 1972 J. Lichbown traced the critical work on this enormously popular medieval work, and compared the prose and metrical versions without mentioning Nassington's imputed authorship.[27]

The <u>Spiritus Guydonis</u> recounts the ghostly appearance of Guy to his wife in which he tells her he is in Purgatory, and then describes its nature. Immediately after the apparition, she informs the priest, who helps her question Guy on the pains of Purgatory, and expiation of sin, and the power to mediate for souls in Purgatory. Guy's wife agrees to live chastely to expedite his entrance into heaven. Many of the doctrinal discussions, included as Guy's responses to the interrogation, are such commonplaces, that they provide no trace of individual authorship, such as the necessity of doing penance for sin (35-36), the power of Christ as a shield against the devil (701-702), the importance of doing all things for God (884-936), and the evil of committing sins against the Holy Spirit (936-960).

It is unlikely that a man of Nassington's intellectual stature, rooted in the patristic tradition, the compiler of an original tract based on the grace of the Gifts of the Holy Spirit, would produce a version of a popular poem based on a ghostly apparition. Moreover, Nassington uses authorities--scripture, orthodox church pronouncements, prominent historical and ecclesiastical figures--to convey the essential doctrine of the institutional church and to promote the spiritual development of its members.

Like the other minor poems in MS. Cotton Tiberius E. VII, the *Spiritus Guydonis* bears no evidence of Nassington. This conclusion challenges Horstmann, but follows the manuscript work of Nevanlinna and Venetia Nelson, who found that the interference of the Tiberius scribe makes the question of determining authorship inconclusive. Furthermore, the two works attributed to Nassington by manuscript evidence, the *Speculum Vitae* and the *Tractatus et Trinitate et Unitate*, reveal that Nassington is original in compiling the fruits of his scholarship, and a mystic, whose experience in prayer graces the language of his texts with affection and joy.

NOTES

[1] British Museum, Department of Manuscripts, Catalogue of the Additions to the MSS of the British Museum, 1888-93, pp. 156-57.

[2] C. Horstmann, ed., Yorkshire Writers, Richard Rolle of Hampole An English Father of the Church and His Followers, Vol. II (Swan Sonnenschein, 1886), p. 283.

[3] Catalogue of the Additions to the MSS of the British Museum, 1888-93, "Additional 33,995," p. 156.

[4] J. E. Wells, A Manual of the Writings in Middle English, 1050-1400, II (New Haven: Yale University Press, 1916), pp. 463-64; Carleton Brown and Russell Hope Robbins, Index of Middle English Verse (Oxford: Clarendon Press, 1943,), p. 40.

[5] C. Horstmann, ed., II, p. 334. All quotations from the minor works will be taken from Horstmann's edition of Yorkshire Writers.

[6] Wolfgang Riehle, The Middle English Mystics, trans. Bernard Standring (London: Routledge & Kegan Paul, 1981), p. 87.

[7] Horstmann, ed., II, p. 274.

[8] H. L. D. Ward, Catalogue of Romances in the Dept. of MSS in the British Museum, I-II, London, 18, 1883-93, p. 740.

[9] Horstmann, ed., II, p. 334.

[10] Francis Foster, The Northern Passion, Fr. Text, Variants, and Fragments (EETS, 147, 1916), p. 5.

[11] Wells, II, pp. 463-64.

[12] Saara Nevanlinna, ed., The Northern Homily Cycle (Helsinki: Societe Neophilologique, 1972), p. 127.

[13] Nevanlinna, ed., p. 136-37.

[14] Venetia Nelson, "Problems of Transcription in the *Speculum Vitae* MSS," *Scriptorium*, 31 (1977), p. 255.

[15] Horstmann, ed., II, p. 334.

[16] Brown and Robbins, II, p. 40.

[17] In Nevanlinna, p. 13, n.1.

[18] In Nevanlinna, p. 13, n.1.

[19] Horstmann, ed., II, p. 334.

[20] Horstmann, ed., II, p. 334.

[21] *Archiv für das Studium Neuren Sprache und Literature*, 211 (Dec., 1974), pp. 300-08.

[22] Horstmann, ed., II, p. 334.

[23] Blake, p. 301.

[24] Hope Emily Allen, *Writings Ascribed to Richard Rolle and Materials for his Biography* (New York: Heath, 1927), pp. 261-62.

[25] Horstmann, ed., II, p. 334.

[26] Nevanlinna, p. 13, n.1.

[27] J. Lichbown, "A Shorter Version of 'Gast of Gy,'" *Modern Language Review* 47, (1952), pp. 323-29.

CHAPTER VI

CONCLUSION

In <u>Literary History of England</u>, Alfred Baugh raised these questions about the <u>Speculum Vitae</u>: "We cannot feel sure of the date, identity of the author, or the immediate source of the poem."[1] My research provides evidence to resolve these uncertainties. Chapter I establishes Nassington's identity, Chapter II his dates and sources, and Chapter V his canon. The biographical data I have ammased on William of Nassington and his ecclesiastical family in York indicates that he is the probable author of the <u>Speculum Vitae</u>. My discovery of the transcription of Archbishop Zouche's appointment of Nassington in 1354 from Exeter as York official and visitor resolves the crux of his identity. The dates of Nassington's life correspond with the certificate in MMS. Cambridge Il.i., Bodleian 445, and Caius College 160, which establishes 1384 as the <u>terminus ad quem</u> for the <u>Speculum Vitae</u>.

Chapters III and IV, a textual analysis of the <u>Speculum Vitae</u>, indicate that it is a didactic work drawing its theology and structure from traditional sources--Augustine, Gregory of Nyssa, Ambrose, Irenaeus, Hilary, Cyprian, Tertullian, Origen, and Thomas. Nassington's synthesis of patristic doctrine meets the demands of the reform movement. This doctrine is also the foundation for his treatment of the three stages of spiritual growth, disclosing the prayerful insight of his rich interior life. Nassington's treatise on perfection stems from his own personal prayer, as any spiritual writing reflects the experience of the author, as well as from scriptural sources. The autobiographical traces of Nassington, as mystic touched by moments of lyric prayer, especially in response to the grace of the Gifts of the Holy Spirit, are identifiable in the <u>Tractatus de Trinitate et Unitate</u>, but not in the other minor poems which Horstmann originally ascribed to Nassington. The colophon in MSS. Royal 17. c. viii and Hatton 19 attributing the <u>Speculum Vitae</u> to Nassington and the incipits in MS. B. L. Additional 33995, naming Nassington as author of the <u>Tractatus</u>, are manuscript evidence to verify his canon.

My investigation of William of Nassington's life and canon has pointed to the need for additional scholarship: a critical edition of his works, comparative studies with continental manuals and English works, (such as Hilton's <u>Scale of Perfection</u>) sources and derivations, contextual studies of the Nassington ecclesiastics, and further studies of the intrinsic leterary art of the <u>Speculum Vitae</u>. My own ongoing research interest will be to explore Nassington's possible debt to Waldeby's sermons, for Waldeby was well-known for his courses on preaching in the Augustinian monastery in York. A study of Nassington, Waldeby, and Abbot Thomas, who comprised the intellectual epicenter of York in the middle of the fourteenth century, promises significant outcomes. Editions of the Registers of William

Zouche would give a focused historical setting for Nassington's activity at the time of the Speculum Vitae. Like Robert Grosseteste, Nassington was a canonist, but his contribution to late medieval writing has been overlooked.

Analogues of the Speculum Vitae and the Tractatus de Trinitate et Unitate need to be studied, and line-by-line comparisons made of similar sections, such as the Somme le Roi, the Prick of Conscience, and Book of Vice and Virtue. Critical editions of the Waldeby Pater Noster tracts and of his sermons are needed to conduct and to study their relation to Nassington's work. Derivative texts of the Speculum Vitae need to be compared with Nassington's original work. These include the four Middle English Mirrors, the De Utilitate, and the Desert of Religion. Investigating currents of St. Bernard's mystical theology and of St. Thomas' scholasticism in the Speculum Vitae will provide further insight into Nassington's thought.

Nassington's centrality as a churchman and mystic in fourteenth-century England needs to be reassessed in light of his erudition, orthodoxy, and widespread audience. Hope Emily Allen did not recognize the Speculum Vitae as a mystical text, though it presents a doctrine and a way of perfection for the ordinary devout Englishman. Nassington's writing does not have the idosyncratic flamboyance of Richard Rolle or Margery Kempe, nor has it commanded the modern scholarly interest in Julian of Norwich and the author of the Cloud of Unknowing. The Speculum

Vitae presents a practical spirituality for a learned and general audience of laity and religious, dedicated to the institutional church, and intent upon spiritual advancement. For these reasons, William of Nassington is a speculum of orthodox fourteenth-century religious England. And the Speculum Vitae is a significant summa of doctrine, a treatise on moral perfection, and a mystical work which contains a wealth of content for further study. Furthermore, Nassington's writing is a witness to the richness of his knowledge of faith, his sensitivity to the human condition, and his response to the grace given all Christians. He is an original thinker who assimilated doctrine and moral theology, presenting it through the experience of his own heart.

William of Nassington is also a speculum of the theology of the via mystica as it flourished in fourteenth-century England, for the Speculum Vitae testifies to the wonder of humankind created in the image of God, the redemption of Christ's passion and death, and the grace of the Holy Spirit to restore the soul to the Imago Dei on its pilgrimage to supernatural glory.

Perhaps Nassington's description of his work, the action of his life that is the fruit of contemplation, is the most valid tribute to his accomplishment:

> Willim saule of Nassington
> Pat gaf his als to fully besly
> Night and day to grete study.

NOTES

[1] New York: Appleton-Century-Crofts, 1948, p. 205. n. 1.

BIBLIOGRAPHY

"Account Rolls of the Dewsbury Rectory, 1348-1356." The Yorkshire Archeological Journal, 23 (1911), 352-92.

Ackerman, Robert W. Backgrounds to Medieval English Literature. New York: Random House, 1966.

Alford, John A. "Biblical Imitatio in the Writings of Richard Rolle," English Literary History, 40 (Spring, 1973), 1-23.

Allen, E. J., ed. "Somme des Vices et Vertues, Part II," Diss. University of North Carolina, 1951.

Allen, Hope Emily. "The Authorship of the Prick of Conscience," Studies in English and Comparative Literature. Boston: Ginn, 1910, 115-70.

⸺. "The Desert of Religion: Addendum." Archiv für das Studium der Neueren Sprachen und Literaturen, 127 (1911), 388-90.

⸺. "A Note on the Lamentation of Mary." Modern Philology, 14 (1916-17), 155-56.

⸺. "The Speculum Vitae: An Addendum." PMLA, 32, (1917), 133-62.

⸺. "Two Middle English Translations from the Anglo-Norman." Modern Philology, 13 (1918), 741-45.

⸺. Writings Ascribed to Richard Rolle, Hermit of Hampole, and Material for His Biography. MLA Monograph Series 3. New York: Heath, 1927.

Allen, Hope Emily, ed. The English Writings of Richard Rolle Hermit of Hampole. Oxford: Clarendon Press, 1931.

Arnould, E. J., ed. Le manuel des peches. Paris, 1940.

Arntz, Mary Luke. "Pe Holy Boke Gratia Dei: An Edition with Commentary." Diss. Fordham University, 1961.

Bateson, F. W., ed. Cambridge Bibliography of English Literature. New York: Macmillan, 1941.

Baugh, Alfred C., ed. A Literary History of England. New York: Appleton-Century-Crofts, 1948.

Blake, N. F. "The Form of Living in Prose and Poetry." Archiv für das Studium der Neueren Sprache und Literature, 211 (1974), 300-08.

_____. Middle English Religious Prose. York Medieval Texts. London: Edward Arnould; and Evanston, Ill.: Northwestern University Press, 1972.

Bloomfield, Morton W., et al. Incipits of Latin Works on the Virtues and Vices 1100-1500 A.D.: Including a Section of Incipits of Works on the Pater Noster. Cambridge, Mass.: The Medieval Academy of America, 1979.

Bradley, Ritamary. "Backgrounds of the Title Speculum in Medieval Literature." Speculum, 29 (1954), 100-15.

Brayer, Edith. "Contentu, Structure et Combinaisons du Miroir du Monde et de la Somme le Roi." Romania, 79 (1958), 1-38.

Brentano, Robert. "Late Medieval Changes in the Administration of Vacant Suffragan Dioceses: Province of York." The Yorkshire Archeological Journal, 38, (1955), 396-503.

_____. Two Churches: England and Italy in the Thirteenth Century. Princeton: Princeton University Press, 1968.

Brown, Carleton. A Register of Middle English and Didactic Verse. Oxford: Clarendon Press, 1916.

Brown, Carleton and Rossell Hope Robbins. Index of Middle English Verse. Oxford: Clarendon Press, 1943.

Bullett, Gerald. The English Mystics. London: Michael Joseph, 1950.

Bulter, Cuthbert. Western Mysticism; The teaching of Augustine, Gregory and Bernard on Contemplation and the Contemplative Life; London: Constable and Co., 1922, 1924; 2nd ed. with Afterthoughts," 1927, 1951; New York: E. P. Dutton, 1924; 2nd ed. 1951.

The Cambridge History of English Literature. Eds. A. W. Ward and A. R. Waller. Cambridge, 1907-; rpt. New York: Macmillan, 1933, Vol. 2.

Catalogue of the Additions to the Manuscripts of the British Museum: London, 1841-1945.

Catalogue of the Manuscripts in the Cottonian Library, Comp. J. Planta. London, 1802.

Catalogue of Romances in the Department of Manuscripts in the British Museum. I-II. Ed. H. L. D. Ward; III. Ed. J. A. Herbert. London, 1883-93, 1910.

Catalogue of Western Manuscripts in the Old Royal and King's Collection. Eds. George F. Warner and Julius P. Gilson, 1921. Vol. 2.

Cayre, F., trans. Manual of Patrology and History of Theology, 2 vols. H. Howitt. Paris: Desclee, 1940.

Chambers, R. W. On the Continuity of English Prose from Alfred to More and his School. London: Oxford University Press, 1932.

Cheney, Christopher R. English Bishops' Chanceries 1100-1250. Manchester: Manchester University Press, 1950.

_____. English Synodalia of the Thirteenth Century. Oxford, 1941.

_____. "Legislation of the Medieval English Church, Part I." Historical Review, 198 (1935), 193-224.

_____. Medieval Texts and Studies. Oxford: Clarendon Press, 1973.

Churchill, Irene. Canterbury Administration. I. London, 1933.

Coleman, Thomas W. English Mystics of the Fourteenth Century. Westport, Conn.: Greenwood Press Publishers, 1971, rpt, London: Epworth Press, 1938.

Colledge, Edmund, ed. and trans. The Mediaeval Mystics of England. New York: Charles Scribner's Sons, 1961.

Collins, Joseph B. Christian Mysticism in the Elizabethan Age With its Background in Mystical Methodology. New York: Octogon, 1971.

Comper, Frances M. The Life or Richard Rolle, Together with an Edition of his English Lyrics. London and Toronto: J. M. Dent, 1928; rpt. New York: Barnes and Noble, 1969.

Cumming, William P. "A Middle English MS in the Bibliotheque Ste. Genevieve Paris." PMLA, 42, (1927), 862-64.

Deansley, Margaret, ed. *The Incendium Amoris of Richard Rolle of Hampole*. Manchester: Manchester University Press, 1915.

_____. *The Lollard Bible and Other Medieval Biblical Versions*. Cambridge, Cambridge University Press, 1920.

Dictionary of National Biography. Eds. Leslie Stephen and Sidney See. London, 1882-; rpt. London: Oxford University Press, 1967-68. Vols. 14, 23.

Dictionnaire de spiritualité ascetique et mystique doctrine et histoire. Eds. Marcel Viller et al. 10 vols. 1937-79.

Doyle, A. I. "A Survey of the Origins and Circulation of the Theological Writings in English in the 14th, 15th, and Early 16th Centuries." Diss. Downing College, 1953.

Emden, A., ed. *A Biographical Register of the University of Oxford to A. D. 1500*, Oxford: Clarendon Press, 1958, Vol. 2.

Extracts from the Account Rolls of the Abbey of Durham, II. Surtees Society Publications, 100 (1898).

Forshaw, Helen P., ed. *Edmund of Abingdon Speculum Religiosorum and Speculum Ecclesie*. London: Oxford University Press, 1973. Foster, Francis, ed. *The Northern Passion French Text, Variants and Fragments, etc.* EETS O.S. 147, 1916.

Fournier, Paul. *Les Officialities au Moyen Age*. Paris: E. Plon, 1880.

Fowler, R. E. *Une source française des poèmes de Gower*. Macon: Protat Freres, 1905.

Francis, Nelson W. *The Book of Vices and Virtues: A fourteenth Century English Translation of the Somme le Roi of Lorens D' Orleans*. Edited from three extant manuscripts. EETS O.S. 217, 1942.

_____. "The Original of the *Ayenbite of Inwyt*." *PMLA*, 52 (1937), 893-95.

Gasquet, Abbot Francis A. *The Eye of the Reformation*. London: George Bell, 1905.

Gibbs, M. and J. Lang. *Bishops and Reform, 1215-1272*. Oxford, 1934.

Goldthorp, L. M. "Franciscans and Dominicans in Yorkshire." *The Yorkshire Archeological Journal*, 32 (1936), 265-428.

Gradon, Phyllis, ed. <u>Dan Michel's Ayenbite of Inwyt or Remorse of Conscience</u>: Richard Morris's Transcription now newly collated with the unique Manuscript British Museum MS, Arundel 57. EETS O.S. 23, 1886, reissued 1965.

Gross, Charles. <u>The Sources and Literature of English History from the Earliest Times to about 1485</u>. London: Longmans, Green, 1915.

Gunn, Agnes David. "Accidia and Prowess in the Vernon Version of Nassyngton's <u>Speculum Vitae</u>: An Edition of the Text and a Study of the Ideas." Diss. University of Pennsylvania, 1969.

Gwynn, Aubrey. <u>The English Austin Friars</u>. Oxford, 1940.

Hartung, Albert E., ed. <u>A Manual of the Writings in Middle English 1050-1500</u>. New Haven; Connecticut Academy of Arts and Sciences, 1972. Vol. 2.

Hilton, Walter. <u>The Scale of/or Ladder of Perfection</u>. Ed. J. B. Dalgairnes. New York: Art and Book Company, 1901.

<u>Historians of the Church of York</u>, 3 Vols. Ed. James Raine, Rolls Series, 1879-94.

Hodgson, Geraldine E. <u>The Sanity of Mysticism: A Study of Richard Rolle</u>. London: Faith Press, 1926, rpt. Forcroft, Pa.: Forcroft Library Editions, 1977.

_____. <u>Some Minor Works of Richard Rolle with the Privity of the Passion by St. Bonaventura</u>. London: Watkins, 1923.

Hodgson, Phyllis, ed. <u>The Cloud of Unknowing and the Book of Privy Counselling</u>. EETS O.S. 218, 1944; rpt. London: Oxford University Press, 1973.

_____, "Ignorancia Sacerdotum:" A Fifteenth-Century Discourse on the Lambeth Constitutions. <u>RES</u>, 24 (1948), p. 1-11.

_____. <u>Three 14th Century English Mystics</u>. London: Longmans, green, 1967.

Holmstedt, Gustaf. <u>Speculum Christiani: A Middle English Religious Treatise of the 14th Century</u>. EETS O.S. 118, 1933.

Horstmann, Carl, ed. <u>Yorkshire Writers, Richard Rolle of Hampole: An English Father of the Church, and His Followers</u>, 2 vols. London: Swan Sonnenschein, 1895, 1896.

Konrath, M. "Review of Library of Early English Writers, Yorkshire Writers, C. Horstmann." Archiv für das Studium der Neueren Sprache und Literature (1897), 158-67.

Krapp, George Philip. The Rise of English Literary Prose. New York: Frederick Ungar, 1915.

Lagorio, Valerie. "The Legend of Joseph Arimathea in Middle English Literature." Diss. Sanford University, 1966.

_____. "Social Responsibility and the Medieval Woman Mystics on the Continent." Analecta Cartusiana, 1982.

Legge, M. Dominica. "St. Edmund's 'Merure de Seinte Eglise.'" Modern Language Review, 23 (1928), 475-76.

_____. "Wanted: An Edition of St. Edmund's 'Merure.'" Modern Philology, 54 (1959), 72-74.

Le Neve, John. Fasti Ecclesiae Anglicanae, 1300-1541, 12 vols. University of London, Institute of Historical Research: Athlone Press, 1962-67.

Liegey, Gabriel M. "The Canticum Amoris of Richard Rolle." Traditio, 12 (1956), 369-91.

_____. "Richard Rolle's Carmen Prosaicum, an Edition and a Commentary." Medieval Studies, 19 (1957), 15-36.

Lightbown, J. "A Shorter Version of 'Gast of Gy.'" Modern Language Review, 47 (1952), 323-29.

Little, A. G. Grey Friars at Oxford. Oxford, 1892.

_____. Initia operum latinorum. Manchester, 1904.

MacCracken, Henry Noble. "Quixley's Ballades Royal (?1402)." The Yorkshire Archeological Journal, 20 (1908), 33-39.

Madigan, Mary Felicitas. The Passio Domini Theme in the Works of Richard Rolle: His Personal Contribution in its Religious, Cultural, and Literary Context. Salzburg: Institute fur Englische Sprache Und Literatur, 1978.

Manning, Stephen. Wisdom and Number, Toward a Critical Appraisal of the Middle English Religious Lyric. Lincoln: University of Nebraska Press, 1962.

Meech, Sanford B., and Hope Emily Allen, eds. The Book of Margery Kempe. EETS O. S. 212. London, 1940; London: Oxford Univ. Press, 1961.

Hübner, Walter. "The Desert of Religion." Archiv für das Studium der Neueren Sprache und Literature, 126 (1911), 58-74.

Hulme, William H. "A Valuable Middle English Manuscript." Modern Philology, 4 (1906), 67-73.

Hunt, William. The English Church in the Middle Ages. New York: Randolf, n.d.

Hussey, M. "The Petitions of the Pater Noster in Medieval English Literature." Medium Aevum, 27 (1958), 8-16.

Ingè, William Ralph. Studies of English Mystics. London: John Murray, 1907.

The Inventories and Account Rolls of the Benedictine Houses or Cells: Jarrow and Monk-Wearmouth in the Country of Durham, Surtees Society Publications, 29 (1854).

Jepsen, John J., trans. St. Augustine: The Lord's Sermon on the Mount. Westminister, Maryland: Newman Press, 1948.

Jolliffee, Peter S. A Check-List of Middle English Prose Writings of Spiritual Guidance. Toronto: Pontifical Institute of Mediaeval Studies, 1974.

Julian of Norwich. The Revelations of Divine Love. Trans., James Walsh. St. Meinrad, Ind.: Abbey Press, 1975.

Kieckhefer, Richard. "Mysticism and Social Consciousness in the Fourteenth Century." Revue de L'Universite d'Ottawa/ University of Ottawa Quarterly, 48 (1978), 179-86.

Kirchberger, Clare. "Bodleian Manuscripts Relating to the Spiritual Life, 1500-1750." Bodleian Library Record, 3 (1951), 155-64.

Knowles, David. The English Mystical Tradition. London: Burns & Oates, and New York: Harper and Brothers, 1961.

Knowlton, Sr. Mary Authur. The Influence of Richard Rolle and of Julian of Norwich on the Middle English Lyrics. The Hague: Mouton, 1973.

Kölbing, E. "Zu Richard Rolle de Hampole." Englische Studien, 3 (1880), 406.

Memorials of Beverely Minster: the Chapter Act Book of the Collegiate Church of St. John of Beverley, A.D. 1286-1347. Ed. A. F. Leach. Surtees Society Publications. I, 98 (1897); II, 108 (1903).

Michel, Dan. Ayenbite of Inwyt or Remorse of Conscience. Ed. Richard Morris. EETS O. S. 23, 1886.

Moorman, John R. H. Church Life in England in the Thirteenth Century. Cambridge: University Press, 1955.

Morgan, Margery, M. "Meditations on the Passion Ascribed to Richard Rolle," Medium Aveum, 12 (1953), 93-103.

Morrill, Georgiana Lea, ed. Speculum Gy de Warewyke, An Early English Poem. EETS E. S. 75, 1898.

Morris, Richard, ed. Cursor Mundi. EETS O. S., 57, 59, 62, 66, 68, 99, 100 (1874-93).

Nelson, Venetia. "Cot. Tiberius E. VII: A Manuscript of the Speculum Vitae." English Studies, 59 (1978), 97-113.

———. "An Introduction to the Speculum Vitae." Essays in Literature (Denver) 2, (1974), 75-102.

———. "Problems of Transcription in the Speculum Vitae MSS." Scriptorium, 31 (1977), 254-59.

———. "The Vernon and Simeon Copies of the Speculum Vitae," English Studies, 57 (1976), 390-94.

Nevanlinna, Saara, ed. The Northern Homily Cycle: The Expanded Version in MSS Harley 4196 and Cotton Tiberius E. vii. From Advent to Septuagesima. Helsinki: Societe Neophilologique, 1972.

"On the Form of Confession." Horae Eboracenses. Surtees Society, 132 (1920), 165-67.

Owen, Dorothy M., ed. John Lydford's Book. London: HMSO, 1974.

Owst, Gerald R. Literature and Pulpit in Medieval England: A Neglected Chapter in the History of English Letters and of the English People. Cambridge: Cambridge University Press, 1933; rpt. New York: Barnes and Noble, 1966.

———. Preaching in Medieval England: An Introduction to Sermon Manuscripts of the period c. 1350-1450. Cambridge: Cambridge University Press, 1926.

Pantin, William A. The English Church in the Fourteenth Century. Cambridge: Cambridge University Press, 1955.

Peacock, Edward, ed. Instructions for Parish Priests by John Myrc. EETS O. S. 31, 1868.

Pepler, Conrad. The English Religious Heritage. St. Louis: Herder, 1968.

Perry, George C., ed. English Prose Treatises of Richard Rolle of Hampole. EETS O. S. 20, 1981.

_____. Religious Pieces in Prose and Verse Edited from Robert Thornton's MS (Cir. 1440). EETS O. S. 26, 1887, 1889.

Petersen, Kate O. The Sources of the Parson's Tale. Radcliffe College Monograph, 12. Boston: Ginn, 1901.

Petry, Ray C., ed. Late Medieval Mysticism. Library of Christian Classics. Vol. 13. Philadelphia: Westminister Press, 1957.

_____. "Social Responsibility and the Late Medieval Mystics." Church History, 21 (1952), 3-9.

Pfander, H. G. "The Medieval Friars and Some Alphabetical Reference Books for Sermons," Medium Aevum, 3 (1934), 19-29.

_____. "Some Medieval Manuals of Religious Instruction in England and Observations on Chaucer's Parson's Tale." JEGP, 35 (1936), 243-58.

Post, R. R. The Modern Devotion: Confrontation with Reformation and Humanism. Leiden: Brill, 1968.

Poulain, A. The Graces of Interior Prayer: A Treatise on Mystical Theology. Trans. Leonard L. Yorke Smith. London: Routledge & Kegan Pual, 1951.

Pourrat, P. Christian Spirituality in the Middle Ages. Trans. S. P. Jacques. London, 1924.

Powell, Lawrence Fitzroy, ed. The Mirrour of the Blessed Lyf of Jesu Christ. Oxford: Clarendon Press, 1908.

Power, Eileen. Medieval English Nunneries, c. 1275-1535. Cambridge: Cambridge University Press, 1922.

The Register of John de Grandisson, Bishop of Exeter, 1327-1369. 3 vols. Ed. F. C. Hingeston-Randolph. London, George Bell, 1899.

The Register of Thomas Corbridge Archbishop of York, 1300-1304.
Eds. W. Brown and A. H. Thompson. Publications of the Surtees Society, I, 138, (1925); II, 141, (1928).

The Register of William Greenfield, Archbishop of York, 1306-1315.
Eds. W. Brown and A. H. Thompson. Publications of the Surtees Society, I, 145, (1931); II, 149, (1934); III, 151, (1936); IV, 152, (1937); V, 153, (1938).

The Registers of John Romeyn and Henry Newark, Archbishops of York, 1286-1296, 1296-1299. Ed. W. Brown. Publications of the Surtees Society, I, 123, (1913); II, 128, (1916).

Riehle, Wolfgang. The Middle English Mystics. Trans. Bernard Standring. London: Routledge and Kegan Paul, 1981.

Ritson, Joseph, ed. Bibliographia Poetica: A Catalog of English Poets of the 12th, 13th, 14th, 15th, and 16th Centuries; With a short account of their work. London: Rowark, 1802.

Robbins, Harry Wolcott, ed. Saint Edmund's "Merure de Seinte Eglise:" An Early Example of Rhythmical Prose. Lewisburg, Pa.: University Print Shop, 1923.

Robbins, Rossell Hope. "The Gurney Series of Religious Manuscripts." PMLA 54 (1939), 369-90.

_____. "Popular Prayers in Middle English Verse." Modern Philology, 36 (May, 1939), 337-50.

Robbins, Rossell Hope and John L. Cutler. Supplement to the Index of the Middle English Verse. Lexington, Ky.: University of Kentucky Press, 1965.

Rowland, Beryl, ed. Chaucer and Middle English Studies in Honour of Rossell Hope Robbins. London: George Allen and Unwin, 1974.

Russell, G. H. "Vernacular Instruction of the Laity in the Later Middle Ages in England: Some Texts and Notes." Journal of Religious History, 2 (1962), 98-119.

Sajavaara, Kari. "The Relationship of the Vernon and Simeon Manuscripts," Neuphilogische Mitteilungen, 68 (1967), 428-39.

Simmons, T. F. and H. E. Nolleth, eds. Lay Folks' Catechism. EETS O. S. 118, 1901.

Smeltz, John W. "Speculum Vitae: An Edition of British Museum Manuscript Royal 17 C, viii." Diss. Duquesne University, 1977.

Smith, Waldo E. Episcopal Appointments and Patronage in the Reign of Edward III. Chicago: American Society of Church History, 1938.

Southern, R. W. The Making of the Middle Ages. London, 1953.

Stover, Edna V. "A Myrour to Lewde Men and Wymmen." Diss. Pennsylvania University, 1951.

_____. "Myrour to Lewde Men and Wymmen, A Note on a Recently Acquired Manuscript." University of Pennsylvania Library Chronicle, 16 (1950), 81-86.

Summary Catalogue of Western Ms. in the Bodleian Library at Oxford, 2, Pt. I. Ed. F. A. Madan. Oxford: Clarendon Press, 1922.

Tanquerary, A. The Spiritual Life; A Treatise on Ascetical and Mystical Theology. Trans. Herman Branderis. Tournai: Descless and Co., 1930.

Thomas Aquinas. Summa Theologiae, Vol. 24. The Gifts of the Spirit (1a2ae. 68-70). Trans. Edward C. O'Connor. New York: McGraw-Hill, 1973.

Thompson, A. Hamilton. The English Clergy and Their Organization in the Later Middle Ages. Oxford: Clarendon Press, 1947.

_____. "The Registers of the Archbishops of York," The Yorkshire Archaeological Journal, 32 (1936), 245-320.

_____. "Some Letters From the Register of William Zouche, Archbishop of York," Historical Essays in Honour of James Tait. Ed. J. G. Edwards. Manchester: Printed for the Subscribers, 1933, 327-43.

Thomson, S. Harrison. The Writings of Robert Grosseteste, Bishop of Lincoln, 1235-1253. Cambridge: Cambridge University Press, 1940.

Tuma, George Wood. The Fourteenth-Century English Mystics: A Comparative Analysis, 2 vols. Salzburg: Institut für Englische Sprache und Literatur, 1977.

Tysor, A. B. ed. "Somme des Vices et Vertues, Part I." Diss., University of North Carolina, 1949.

Ullman, J. "Studien zu Richard Rolle de Hampole." Englische Studien 7 (1884), 415-72.

Underhill, Evelyn, ed. *The Scale of Perfection*. London: J. M. Watkins, 1923.

Varnhagen, Hermann. "Dan Michel's *Ayenbite of Inwit*." *Englische Studien*, 1 (1877), 379-423.

Warton, Thomas. *History of English Poetry from the Twelfth to the Close of the Sixteenth Century*, 4 vols. Ed. W. Hazlitt. London: Reeves and Turner, 1871, rpt., Hildesheim: George Olms Verlagsbuchhandlung, 1968.

Watkin, Aelred. "An English Medieval Instruction Book for Novices." *Downside Review*, 42 (1939), 477-88.

Watson, G. "M. E. Poem: Identification." *Notes and Queries*, (November 22, 1924), 371.

Weber, Sarah Appleton. *Theology and Poetry in the Middle English Lyric. A Study of Sacred History and Aesthetic Form*. Columbus: Ohio State University Press, 1969.

Wells, John E., et al. *A Manual of the Writings in the Middle English, 1050-1400*. New Haven: Yale University Press, 1916.

White, Helen C. *English Devotional Literature (Prose) 1600-1640*. University of Wisconsin Studies in Language and Literature, 29. Madison: University of Wisconsin, 1931.

——. *Tudor Books of Private Devotion*. Madison: University of Wisconsin Press, 1951.

Whiting, C. E. "Excavations at Hampole Priory." *The Yorkshire Archeological Journal*, (1937), 204-12.

——. "Richard Rolle of Hampole." *The Yorkshire Archeological Journal*, (1948), 5-23.

Wilkins, D. *Concilia Magnae Britanniae et Hiberniae*. London, 1937.

Wilmart, A. *Auteurs spirituels et textes dévots du moyen âge*. Paris, 1932.

Wiltshire, Alan. "The Latin Primacy of St. Edmund's Mirror of Holy Church." *Modern Language Review*, 71 (1976), 500-12.

Wolters, Clifton, ed. *The Cloud of Unknowing*. Penguin: Harmondsworth, England, 1961.

Wood-Legh, Kathleen L. *Studies in Church Life in England under Edward II*. Cambridge: Cambridge University Press, 1934.

Woolf, Rosemary. *The English Lyric in the Middle Ages*. Oxford: Clarendon Press, 1968.

Young, Karl. "Instructions for Parish Priests," *Speculum*, 11 (1936), 224-31.

Zeeman, Elizabeth. "Continuity in Middle English Devotional Prose," *Journal of English and Germanic Philology*, 55 (2956), 417-22.

Zupita, J. "Zu Angfang des *Speculum Vitae*." *Englische Studien*, 12 (1889), 468-69.

_____. "Zur Meditacio Ricardi Heremite de Hampole de Passione Domime." *Englische Studien*, 12 (1889), 463-67.

INDEX

Ambrose 147
Abbot of Wardon Abby 25
<u>Administrative History of Medieval England</u> 8
Administration
   archdeacon 9, 15
   auditor 21
   benefice 11, 14, 15, 19, 45, 105
   canon 9-11, 14, 16, 19, 21, 22, 46
   chancellor 15, 19, 63
   civil service bishop 8, 9, 14, 16, 21
   clerk 14, 17, 18, 19, 22, 45
   dean 9
   magister 15, 16, 18, 20, 45
   official 10-15, 18, 19, 108
   parson 11, 22
   prebend 10, 11, 13, 15, 17, 20-21
   precentor 9, 15
   proctor 19, 23, 24
   rector 10, 19
   treasurer 9
   vicar 9-12, 14, 15, 18-20, 51
Affective Prayer 22; See also <u>Speculum Vitae</u>: Illumination
Alexander, King 103
Allen, Hope Emily 1, 24, 40-44, 47, 49, 52, 55, 57, 60, 61, 62, 163
Ambrose 88, 102, 132, 143
<u>Ancrene Riwle</u> 101, 102
<u>Ancrene Wisse</u> 146
Anselm 103, 114, 143
Anselm of Canterbury 114
Archbishops; See John Romeyn, Henry Newark, Thomas Corbridge, John Melton,
   William Zouche, William Greenfield, John Grandisson, John Pecham
Arundel 47
Audience; See <u>Speculum Vitae</u>
Auditor; See Administration
Augustine 53, 57, 58, 78, 99, 100, 103, 114, 132, 141, 145, 152, 169
Austin Friars 6, 16, 52, 62-64
Autobiographical Evidence; See <u>Speculum Vitae</u>
Avarice; See Vice and Virtue
<u>Ayenbite of Inwyt</u> 55-56

Bale 62
<u>Bande of Lovynge</u> 22, 44, 150
Barnstable 14, 15
Baugh, Alfred 169
Beatitudes 46, 57-59; See also <u>Speculum Vitae</u> 100-104
   blessed are the poor 96, 98, 101
   blessed are the meek 96, 98, 101
   blessed are the sorrowful 96, 98, 101
   blessed are those who hunger and thirst 96, 98, 101
   blessed are the merciful 96, 98, 101
   blessed are the clean of heart (purity) 96, 98, 100, 102, 144-145
   blessed are the peacemakers 96, 98, 100, 102, 145

Benedictines 52, 64
Berkshire 51
Bernard 123, 125, 128, 132, 136, 149, 159, 160, 171
Beverley 14, 16
Bevis of Hampton 80
Blake, N. F. 160
Bloomfield, Morton 59
Bodleian; See Manuscripts
Bole 14
Bologna 15
Bonaventure 150
Book of Job 58
Book of Vice and Virtue 50, 171
Bosham 19, 20
Bratton-Clovelly 19
Brentano, Robert 18
Brown, Carlton 17
Brown and Robbins 1, 17, 47, 129, 158
Brunne; See Mannyng, Robert
Burgh, John de 48, 49, 51
Butler 8

Caius College; See Manuscripts
Calendars of Patent and Close Rolls 18, 24, 26
Cambridge 6, 12, 26, 48; See Also Manuscripts
Cambridge Certification 26, 47-50, 66
Cambridge History of English Literature 40
Canon; See Administration
Canterbury 114
Cardinal Virtues; See also Speculum Vitae
Casley 41
Catalog of Romances 47, 155
Catalog of Western Manuscripts 25
Catalog of Royal Manuscripts 41, 62
Catherine of Siena 143
Chancellor; See Administration
Chastity; See Virtue
Chaucer 11
Chichester 19
Chrysostom 143
Civil Service Bishop; See Administration
Cleric; See Administration
Clergy; See Reform
Cloud of Unknowing 6, 125, 142, 143, 171
Colledge, Eric 114
Commandments 51, 56, 61
Commentary on the Pater Noster 62
Confession; See Speculum Vitae
Constitutions 3, 4
Constitutions; See Reform
Corbridge, Thomas 13
Cornwall 19
Cotton Tiberius; See Manuscripts
Councils; See Trent, Lambeth
Creed 52, 61, 63

Counsel; See Gifts
Cursor Mundi 50
Cyprian 58, 103, 132, 169

De Informatione Simplicium 4
De Quinque Seu Septem 59
De Sermone Domini in Monte 57, 98
De Spiritus Guidonis; See Spiritus Guidonis
De Trinitate et Unitate; See Tractatus
De Utilitate 17, 59-61, 171
Dean; See Administration
Desert of Religion 48, 133, 171
Dictionary of National Biography 40
Diocese; See Administration
Dogma 52, 82, 86
Doyle 43, 44, 48-50, 65, 80
Durham 17, 19, 21

Eckhardt, Meister 143
Edward I 14
Edward II 15
Edward III 14, 18, 21
Enarratio in Psalmum 103 53
English Mystics 6-7
Envy; See Vice
Evangelia Dominicalia
Evenhead (Equity); See Virtue
Exeter 25, 28, 106
Facsicule Zizaniorum 63
Fasti 17
Fear; See Vice
First Exposition; See Speculum Vitae
Form of Living 27, 59, 60, 155-157, 160-163
Fortitude; See Gifts
Foster, Francis 1, 155-156
Fourth Lateran Council 2, 3, 7, 50, 54, 61
Fowler, R. E. 52
Francis, Nelson 153
Friendship; See Virtue
Frolich, W. 158

Gast of Guy 163
Gaytrick, John 52
Gifts 89-100
    fear 96-100
    piety 96, 100
    knowledge 96, 98, 100
    fortitude 96, 98
    counsel 96, 98
    understanding 96, 98
    wisdom 96, 98
Gilbertine 54
Gilson 25, 62

Gluttony; See Vice
Gower, John 52
Grabes 53
Grace 85, 11
Grandisson, John 15, 18, 21, 24, 25
Gregory of Nyssa 58, 103, 130, 132, 135, 169
Greenfield, William 4, 10, 13
Grosseteste, Robert 3, 4, 5, 9, 51, 59, 103, 171
Gunn, Agnes David 26, 59, 60
Guy of Warwick 80
Gwynn, Aubrey 62-64

Halliwell 40
Handling Sin 54
Hastings Castle 21
Hatton; See Manuscripts
Hereford 16
Heresy; See Lollard
Hingeston-Randolph, F. C. 107
Hilary 58, 169
Hilton, Walter 6, 114, 125, 142, 143, 150, 170
History of English Poetry 23, 40
Holy Spirit 46, 83
Homilies 63, 80, 155-156
Horstmann 1, 23-24, 46, 61, 149, 154, 155, 159, 160, 163, 170
Humility; See Virtue
Hugh of St. Victor 53, 59
Huntingdon Diocese 14, 16

Imago Dei 53, 58, 78, 90, 94, 112-115, 122, 126, 133, 135
Imago Peccati 114-116
Incendium Amoris 6
Incipientes; See *Speculum Vitae*: purgation
Illumination 76; See also *Speculum Vitae*
Index 1
Innocent III 2, 8
Instructional Texts 39, 50-52, 58
Instructions for Parish Priests 4, 6, 11, 22, 27, 50-52, 76
Invocation; See *Speculum Vitae*
Ireneas of Lyon 58
Isidore 132
Isumbras 80

James the Apostle 132
Jerome 132
John de Hawlyton 17
John de Burgh; See Burgh
John Nassington 13, 14
John, King of England 8
Judas 106
Judica me deus 51
Julian of Norwich 6, 71

Kempe, Margery 6, 171
Kendal 14
Kieckhefer, Richard 143
King Alexander 103
Kirkeby, Margaret 160
Knowledge; See Gifts
Konrath, K. 158

Ladder of Four Rungs 142
Lamentation of St. Mary; See St. Marys Lamentation to St. Bernard 149
Laity 27, 172
Lambeth, Provincial Council 4, 5
Lancaster 19, 22
Langton, Stephen 3
Laud 463; See Manuscripts
Lay Folk's Catechism 52
Le Chateau D'Amour 103
Le Manuel de Peches 54
Le Mireour Du Monde 59
Le Neve 17
Le Somme des Vices et Virtues; See Somme des Vices et Vertues
Lechery; See Vice
Letters 63, 108
Lichbown, J. 164
Lichfield 16
Lilleshall Salop 52
Lincoln 3, 14, 54
Lincoln Cathedral 91; See Manuscripts
Literary History of England 169
Literacy 80, 157
Lives of Saints 8
Lives of the Archbishops of York 61
Lollard 47
London 19
Lorens d'Orleans 54
Lucifer 103
Lull, Raymond 143

Magister; See Administrator
Mannying, Robert 54
Manual des Peches 44
Manuals of Instruction 4, 12, 45, 54, 57, 170
Manuscripts
    Bodleian E. 35, 64
    Bodleian 446 25, 47
    British Library Li 36 49, 55
    British Library Add 15237 60
    British Library Add 33995 150-153, 170
    Cauis College 160 47
    Cauis College Cambridge 61
    Cambridge Li 8 41, 42, 49
    Cambridge University Library 1 Dd 158

    Cotton Tiberius E. VII 1, 44, 46, 65, 156-158, 164-165
    Harley 45   64
    Harley 435   157
    Harley 2260   64, 157
    Harley 4196   64
    Hatton 19   22, 39, 42, 44-45, 48, 61, 170
    Laud 463   158
    Lincoln Cathedral (Thornton) 91, 149-150, 152
    Rawlinson A. 335   180
    Rawlinson Poetry 175   64, 158, 163
    Royal 17 C viii   25, 39, 41, 170
    Simeon 80   157
    Thornton (Vernon)   24-25, 49, 80, 149, 157, 158, 164
    Trinity College Oxford 57   158, 159
Martha and Mary 143
Martin of Tours 131
Mary Magdelen 103
Matthew 100
Meditation 6
Meditatio Beati Bernardi 158
Meditations of the Passion 41
Meekness; See Virtue
Melos Amoris 6
Melton, William 13, 15
Mercy; See Virtue
Middle English Mystics 124
Minot, Lawrence 157
Miroir du Monde 124
Mirour de L'omne 52
Mirror 53, 171
Mirror of Holy Church 65-67
Mirror of Life 1, 55, 61, 64, 65
Modesty; See Virtue
Monastic Schools 12
Moral Purpose; See *Speculum Vitae*
Moralia 58
Morte Arthure 150
Moses 98
Myrour of Life 23, 40, 41
Myrour to Lewde Men and Women 64, 65
Mystics 44, 46, 67, 76, 125
Mystical Union 86, 153-155; See also *Speculum Vitae*
Mysticism 58, 97
Myrk, John 11, 52

Nassington; See John Nassington, Robert Nassington, Thomas Nassington,
   Roger Nassington, William Nassington
Nassington Family 12
Nassington Prebend 17
Nelson, Venetia 47, 49, 65, 155, 165
Nevanlinna, Saara 44, 156, 165
Newark, Henry 13
New Testament; See *Speculum Vitae*
Newton 14, 21
Nicholas of Cusa 143

North Riding 48
Northampton 25
Northants 17
<u>Northern Homily Cycle</u> 1, 27, 44, 149, 155-157
<u>Northern Passion</u> 156
Northgate, Don Michael 55
Nottingham 15, 18
Norwich; See Julian
<u>Novum Opus Dominicale</u> 63

Octovan 80, 150
Oculus Sacerdotis 51, 52
<u>Of Shrift and Penance</u> 54
Official; See Administration
<u>On the Mixed Life</u> 143
<u>On the Trinity and Unity</u> 41
Origen 58, 169
Osmunderle 25
Osmotherly 18
Owst, G. R. 25, 26
Oxford 6, 12, 18, 20
Oxford, Provincial Council 5, 15, 16

Pagula, William 51, 52
Pantin 8
Papacy 107
<u>Paradisio</u> 142
Parson; See Administration
Pastoral Letters; See Reform
<u>Patent and Close Rolls</u> 13, 18
Pater Noster 39, 46, 50, 57-67, 76, 81-86, 97, 101-103, 110, 115, 129, 140, 171
Pater Noster Petitions; See also Askings 101-103
    Hallowed be thy name 96, 110
    Thy kingdom done 96, 110
    Thy will be done 96, 110
    Give us our daily bread 96, 110
    Forgive us our debts 96, 110
    Lead us not into temptation 96, 110
    Deliver us from evil 96, 110
<u>Patrologia Latina</u> 8
Paul 103, 104, 116, 132, 135, 145
<u>Pearl</u> 144
Pecham, Bishop of Canterbury 4, 5, 9
Penance; See Vice
Perfecti; See <u>Speculum Vitae</u>: mystical union
Perry, George 23, 149
Petitions; See Pater Noster Petitions
Petry, Ray 143
Piety; See Gifts
<u>Populi Oculi</u> 48, 51
<u>Planctus Mariae</u> 158-159
Plato 114
Plotinus 114
Pollard, A. F. 24, 40

Prayer; See Speculum Vitae: purgation, illumination, mystical union
Prebend; See Administration
Precentor; See Administration
Prick of Conscience 1, 42, 54, 101, 137, 146, 150, 156, 171
Pride; See Vice
Private of the Passione 150
Proctor; See Administration
Proficientes; See Speculum Vitae: illumination
Provincial Councils; See Reform
Prowess; See Virtue
Prudentius 103
Purgation; See Speculum Vitae

Raine, James 61
Ramsey Abbey 14
Rawlinson Poetry 175; See also Manuscripts
Reading, Provinicial Council 5, 51
Reason; See Speculum Vitae
Rector; See Administration
Reform 2, 16, 22, 27, 44-46, 50, 54, 61, 82, 86, 100, 106, 169
   synods 3
   constitutions 47
   provincial councils 5
   pastoral letters 6
   manuals of instruction 39, 50
   education of clergy 12
   Speculum Vitae 100
Regio Dissimilitudinis 114
Registers 13; See also Romeyn, Newark, Corbridge, Greenfield, Melton, Zouche
Register of John Grandisson 24
Religious Pieces 23, 149
Repertorium Waldeby 63
Revelations of Divine Love 6
Rich, Edmund 5, 66-67, 150, 154
Riehle, Wolfgang 106, 124, 151
Ritson, Joseph 41
Robert Nassington 15
Roger Nassington 16, 17
Rokeby, Richard 41
Rolle, Richard 1, 6, 7, 23, 40, 42-44, 51, 106, 140, 143, 160-163, 171
Roman Curia 21
Romeyn, John 13, 14, 16, 17
Ruysbroeck, John 143

Salisbury 20, 21, 51
Scale of Perfection 114, 142, 150, 170
Schleich, Gustav 163
Scholastic Method 6, 50
Scriptores Illustres Majoris Brytanniae 62
Scripture 63, 67
Second Exposition; See Speculum Vitae
Sempringham 54
Seneca 103
Sermons 63

Simeon; See Manuscripts
Sloth; See Vice
Soberness; See Virtue
Solomon 80
Somme 52, 56
<u>Somme des Vices et Virtues</u> 54, 55-56, 60, 78, 84
<u>Somme le Roi</u> 53, 54-60, 78, 84, 101, 107, 171
<u>Song of Songs</u> 125
South Newbold 14, 16
Southwell 16
Speculum 39, 50, 53-57, 76
<u>Speculum Ecclesiae</u> 5
<u>Speculum Prelatorum</u> 51
<u>Speculum Religiosorum</u> 51
<u>Speculum Vitae</u> 12, 16, 22-27, 39-55
   Articles of the creed 86-87
   Asking 100-102
   Audience 49, 51, 79-82, 162
   Beatitudes 99-100
   Cardinal virtues 86-87, 116
   Commandments 86-87
   Corporal works of mercy 86, 99, 130
   Defense of the vernacular 83
   Eucharist 90, 93
   First exposition 85-89
   Gifts of the Holy Spirit 86, 92, 94; See also Gifts
   Illumination 122-135
   Invocation 82
   Ladder of perfection 103
   Mixed life 113
   Modesty topos 82
   Moral purpose 82
   Mystical Union 136-146, 153-154, 163, 170
   New Testament 87, 99
   Old Testament 87, 99
   Penance, contrition, confession 87, 99
   Prologue 85
   Prowess (word, flesh devil) 87, 92, 117, 121
   Purgation 122-135
   Reason 120
   Sacraments 86
   Second exposition 88-94
   Schema 76, 80-83, 98
   Speculum Image 83-84, 112, 188
   Spiritual works of mercy 86, 99, 130
   Terminus and quem 60, 169
   Theological virtues 86, 87, 116
   Trinity 83, 113, 151
   Third exposition 94-103
   Understanding 84-85, 113; See also Gifts
   Via activa 87, 117
   Via contemplativa 87, 91, 97, 145
   Vices and Virtues 95; See also Vice and Virtue
   Will 87, 99, 115, 116
   Wisdom 17, 99, 123; See also Gifts
Spiritual Works of Mercy; See <u>Speculum Vitae</u>

St. Martin's Altar 14
St. Albans 64
Spiritus Guidonis 27, 147, 155-157, 163-165
St. Mary's Lamentation 27, 155, 157, 158-159
St. Mary Magdalen Hospital 16
Stabat Mater 158
Stamford 17
Statutes 3, 5
Stover, Edna 65
Stowe 15
Strength of Will; See Speculum Vitae
Summa 50-53, 58, 63, 66, 76
Summa Summarum 5, 51, 52
Summa Theologiae 88, 94
Sussex 19, 20
Synod 3, 6, 137; See also Reform

Tauler, John 143
Templum Domini 4, 5, 51, 59, 103
Teresa of Avila 143
Tertullian 58
Theological Virtues 61; See also Speculum Vitae
Third Exposition; See Speculum Vitae
Thomas Aquinas 143, 169
Thomas de la Mare, Abbot 64, 170
Thomas Nassington 15
Thomas, Earl of Lancaster 15
Thompson, A. Hamilton 13
Thoresby 17, 52, 62
Thornton; See Manuscripts
Thornton Romances 40
Tout 8
Tractatus de Trinitae et Unitate 23-24, 27, 39, 40, 149-158, 159, 162-163, 165, 170, 171
Treasurer; See Administration
Trent 12
Trinity 83, 86, 113, 151-154

Ullman, J. 42, 47
Understanding; See Speculum Vitae; See also Gifts

Vernon; See Manuscripts
Via Activa 117; See also Speculum Vitae
Via Mystica; See Speculum Vitae: mystical union
Vernacular; See Speculum Vitae
Vicar General; See Administration
Vice and Virtue 4, 14, 39, 45, 50, 52, 54, 56-60, 76, 78, 84, 86, 89, 91, 96, 99, 100, 103, 110, 112, 114, 117
   Pride 96, 98, 101, 117
   Envy 96, 98, 101, 119
   Wrath 96, 98, 102, 119
   Sloth 96, 98, 101, 120
   Avarice 96, 99, 102-108, 129

Lechery 96, 98, 129, 131-132
    Gluttony 96, 98, 102, 136-138
Virtues
    Humility (meekness) 96, 98, 101, 110, 117
    Friendship 96, 98, 101, 113
    Evenhead (equity) 96, 98, 99, 101, 119
    Prowess 96, 98, 99, 102, 121
    Mercy 96, 99, 101, 103, 131-133
    Chastity 96, 98, 103, 131
    Soberness 96, 98, 103, 138

Waddington, William 54
Waldeby, John 1, 6, 16, 23, 26, 39, 40, 61-63, 145, 170-173
Waldeby, Robert 61, 63
Waldenby, John de 23
Wallensis, Johannes 52, 62
Warden Abbey 25
Ward, H. L. D. 47, 155
Ward and Waller 160
Warner, George F. and Gibson, Julius P. 25, 62
Warton, Thomas 23, 24, 40
Way of Perfection 46, 171; See also <u>Speculum Vitae</u>:
    Purgation, Illumination, Mystical Union
Wells, John E. 1, 16, 47, 151
Weremouth 19
Westmoreland 14
William de Meryet 20
William Melton; See Melton, William
William of Nassington
    biography 17-22
    authorship of <u>Speculum Vitae</u> 22-40
    narration on avarice 103-108
    canon 149-164
    family; See John, John Jr., Robert, Thomas, Roger
William of Pagula 51-52
William of Waddington 54
Wistow 14
Wisdom; See <u>Speculum Vitae</u>: Gifts
World, flesh and devil; See <u>Speculum Vitae</u>
Wrath; See Vice
<u>Writings Ascribed to Richard Rolle</u> 43
Wycliffe 47, 48

Yaxley in Huntington 16
<u>Yorkshire Writers</u> 1
York 1, 12, 14, 15, 18-21, 24-26, 43, 44, 54, 62, 63, 108, 157, 169, 170

Zouche, William 18, 20, 21, 62, 63, 169, 171

David Alan Black

Paul, Apostle of weakness
Astheneia and its Cognates in the Pauline Literature

American University Studies: Series VII
(Theology and Religion). Vol. 3
ISBN 0-8204-0106-4   340 pp.   paperback US $ 27.00

Recommended prices – alterations reserved

The most unique and highly developed concept of weakness in the New Testament is to be found in the writings of the apostle Paul. Essentially, Paul's conception of weakness stands in a dynamic relationship with his Christology. He is defensive of his own infirmities only because a misunderstanding of weakness has led to error concerning the nature and acquisition of divine strength. Paul is strong, but only because he is "in Christ". Otherwise he freely admits to being an apostle of weakness, and in so doing has set forth a powerful rationale for Christians of all ages to glory in their weakness, not merely endure them. Contents: The Weak in Thessalonica – Weakness Language in Galatians – The Pauline Perspective on Weakness – Weakness as a Sign of Humanity – Weakness as the Showplace of God's Might – Paul's Relevance for Today.

PETER LANG PUBLISHING, INC.
62 West 45th Street
USA – New York, NY 10036

Lloyd H. Steffen

Self-Deception and the Common Life

American University Studies: Series VII
(Theology and Religion). Vol. 11
ISBN 0-8204-0243-5   415 pp.   hardback US $ 45.40

Self-Deception and the Common Life investigates the topic of self-deception from three points of view: philosophical psychology, ethics, and theology. Empirical evidence and an "ordinary language" analysis support the case that the linguistic expression 'self-deception' is literally meaningful and that the language of the common life can be trusted. After critically analyzing the cognition, translation, and action accounts, along with the contributions of Freud and Sartre, Steffen proposes a new synthetic "emotional perception" account, one that avoids paradox. Giving attention to relevant moral issues, he argues that self-deception is not immoral, but represents a peculiar form of *akrasia*. Finally, because theologians employ 'self-deception' to describe the cognitive component of sin, Steffen considers the logic of theological self-deception. His study seeks an "intimate acquaintance" with self-deception and exemplifies a method of analysis relevant to constructive theological inquiry.

Contents: "Ordinary language" analysis of self-deception – Accounts: cognitions, translation, action, Sartre, Freud, "emotional perception"–self-deception and *akrasia*–theological self-deception: sin, pride, and Kierkegaard's "sin is despair".

PETER LANG PUBLISHING, INC.
62 West 45th Street
USA – New York, NY 10036

Gregory J. Polan

In the Ways of Justice Toward Salvation
A Rhetorical Analysis of Isaiah 56-59

American University Studies: Series VII
(Theology and Religion). Vol. 13
ISBN 0-8204-0280-X   364 pp.   hardback US $ 46.00

The rediscovery of the importance of literary style and art in biblical writings has encouraged the application of new exegetical methods; among these is rhetorical criticism.
Noted biblical critics in the past have looked upon Isaiah 56-59 as a melange of poems with little structural organization or unity of thought.
Gregory Polan, however, demonstrates that appreciation of poetic style and technique leads to greater understanding of the biblical text; and, by examining recurring motifs and themes, he highlights the unity of these Isaian poems. This is rhetorical criticism at work.
In the Ways of Justice Toward Salvation follows the trend established by renewed interest in the rhetoric of Hebrew poetry.
Contents: Chapter One, Recent pioneering efforts in rhetorical criticism, trends in Isaian interpretation, method of analysis for Isaiah 56-59 – Chapters Two through Five, Verse-by-verse analysis of texts – Chapter Six, Summary of rhetorical devices, thematic structure, and development of motifs.

PETER LANG PUBLISHING, INC.
62 West 45th Street
USA – New York, NY 10036